AF522561

China's Global Ambitions
A Reality Check

China's Global Ambitions

A Reality Check

Edited by

Mohshin Habib

© CHARDIK (38/4, Banglabazar, Dhaka - 1100, Bangladesh)

&

HAR-ANAND PUBLICATIONS PVT LTD (E-49/3, Okhla Industrial Area, Phase-II, New Delhi-110020, Tel.: 41603490, E-mail: info@haranandbooks.com/haranand@rediffmail.com, Shop online at: www.haranandbooks.com)

Printed in India at Vinayak Offset

Acknowledgement

Phenomenal rise of China and its implications across the globe from Asia to Europe to Africa to Americas is today a hotly debated subject across governments, company boardrooms, universities and civil societies.

To capture global presence of China we decided to join hands and bring out this collection of essays by noted experts from USA, Australia, Europe, India, Bangladesh, Japan and Vietnam. We, the publishers of the book, are grateful to each of our 12 contributors who took out time from their busy schedule to make this volume a success. Some of our authors also took risk of articulating their views fearlessly and we remain grateful to them.

We are also grateful to Dipanjan Roy Chaudhury, Diplomatic Affairs Editor, *The Economic Times* who watches China closely and without whose guidancc and inputs, the book would not have been complete.

This book has been a unique experiment as there are few such books anywhere in the world that captures rise of China from the eyes of 12 different authors. We hope that readers will appreciate this volume as much as we did in bringing out this book.

Chardik Publication, Dhaka
Har-Anand Publications, India

Introduction

Perhaps no other topic agitates the contemporary strategic imagination more than the implications of China's rise — not just for the future of the ruling elite in Beijing but also for Asia including India, North America, Africa, Europe, Latin America. In the recent past, apprehension about Chinese President Xi Jinping's ambitions has given way to another sentiment, that China may be inching toward overreach — both economic as well as geopolitical — as public opinion across many Western democracies and even non-Western democracies snowball into China skepticism, if not antagonism. Discomfort on China is on rise even in some authoritarian states.

If superpower status is China's desired goal, there are two roads it might take to try to obtain that. The first is the one that runs through China's neighbourhood – South Asia and the Western Pacific. It should focus on building regional primacy as a springboard to global power. The second road is very different because it seems to defy the historical laws of strategy and geopolitics. This approach focuses on developing China's economic, diplomatic, and political influence on a global scale.

The emerging conventional wisdom holds that China will try to establish global influence by first establishing regional hegemony. As China builds economic power through these efforts, it will sharpen its capacity to convert that power into geopolitical influence including in its neighbourhood in South Asia, SE Asia, East Asia, Eurasia, Pacific, Africa and Latin

America. Even North and Central Americas are not immune from the Chinese influence.

But amid China's expanding global footprint there is growing backlash against Beijing's grand schemes and geostrategic goals across continents. Its human rights records at home are difficult to defend even by non-Western standards. The Belt & Road Initiative are pushing countries towards debt trap rather than providing assistance in improving their infrastructure. The military adventures by PLA have compelled China's neighbours to resist and in number of instances PLA has been forced to retreat. The Chinese designs are more often than reminder of the British East India Company.

To capture China's soaring ambitions and implications of that, **Chardik, a leading publishing house from Bangladesh** has joined hands with **Har-Anand Publications, one of India's leading publishers** to bring this volume that is unique in style as it is a collection of essays by experts from various continents narrating tales of Chinese designs and goals in their respective regions. This book is an attempt to narrate impact implications of the global rise of China with a goal to create informed public opinion.

List of Contributors

Dr. Satoru Nagao is a prominent scholar on Indo-Pacific region, is associated with the US-based Hudson Institute.

Grant Wyeth is a columnist for the noted Asia-Pacific affairs Publication The Diplomat.

Mohshin Habib is a senior Bangladeshi author and journalist.

Alicja Bachulska is a China analyst with Asia Research Centre (War Studies University), Warsaw, Poland.

Kelly Alkhouli is the Director of International Relations Center of Political and Foreign Affairs, Europe.

Duncan Bartlett is a Research Associate at the SOAS China Institute, UK.

Estella C is a Sweden-based roving journalist and China analyst.

Gabriel Lafitte is an Australian who has worked with Tibetans for over 40 years, publisher of a regular blog on Tibetan environmental issues, www.rukor.org.

Dr. Vo Xuan Vinh is with the Institute for Southeast Asian Studies Vietnam Academy of Social Sciences, Hanoi, Vietnam.

Dr Michael Kugelman is Asia Program deputy director and senior associate for South Asia at the Woodrow Wilson International Center for Scholars in Washington, DC, USA.

Dr Shaheli Das is a Sinologist and has been a researcher in several premier think tanks in India and abroad.

Dr. Abhishek Darbey is a Research Associate at Centre for China Analysis & Strategy (CCAS), New Delhi, India.

Contents

Chapter 1

What is Beijing's Plan in the Indo-Pacific?

– Dr. Satoru Nagao

Recently, China has escalated its military activities in many places simultaneously, including in the sea around Japan, Taiwan, the South China Sea, the Indian Ocean, and the Indo-China border area. In response, the United States has stepped up its deterrence efforts, and the US-China competition has escalated. The question that remains is, what does China want? If China dominates all these areas, what can China achieve? To prevent China's aggression, what should we do? Therefore, this chapter focuses on three questions to identify a solution for how to deal with China: (1) What activities is China undertaking in the sea around Japan, Taiwan, the South China Sea, the Indian Ocean, and in the India-China border area? (2) What are China's objectives and what can it achieve if it continues these activities? (3) How can other countries contain China?

I. What Activities is China Undertaking?

(1) The Sea around Japan

Since the 2000s, Beijing has been expanding its military

activities near Japan and countries around the South China Sea. For example, in 2004, a Chinese nuclear attack submarine violated Japan's territorial seas in the East China Sea. China has also been carrying out naval exercises on the Pacific side of Japan since 2008, as shown in Figure 1 below.

Figure 1: China's naval and air activities around Japan

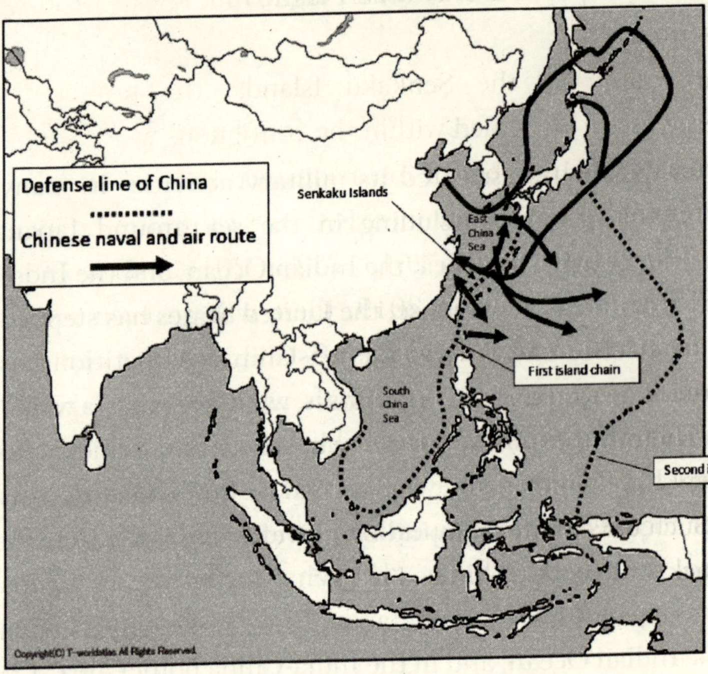

Source: Ministry of Defense of Japan, 2020

The Chinese air force has also been expanding its activities. In 2013, Japan's Ministry of Defense pointed out in a White Paper that, "in FY 2012, the number of scrambles against Chinese aircrafts exceeded the number of those against the Russian aircrafts for the first time." That number further increased to 851 in FY 2016. It decreased to 500 in FY 2017, but the number rose to 638 in FY 2018 and 675 in FY 2019. In FY 2020, the number decreased to 458[1]. But this did not mean China restrained its activities. Indeed, China was so active that it became draining for Japanese fighter pilots to constantly respond. Japan therefore changed its tactics and responded only when the Chinese provocations were serious.

Particularly in the Senkaku Islands, the number of Chinese vessels identified within the contiguous waters began to increase. The number of incursions was only 12 in 2011, but after that they sharply increased to 428 in 2012, 819 in 2013, 729 in 2014,707 in 2015, 752 in 2016, 696 in 2017, and 615 in 2018. And in 2019, there was an even greater jump to 1,097. And the Senkaku Islands are in a strategic location to place pressure on Taiwan, as they are just 170km away. There is information that China is planning to develop the Senkaku Islands to be a place where 20,000 people can live.[2] Such development would also give China a forward base to attack Taiwan.

[1]Joint Staff of Japan's Ministry of Defense, "Statistics on scrambles through FY2020," April 9, 2021, https://www.mod.go.jp/js/Press/press2021/press_pdf/p20210409_03.pdf

[2]Masaya Kato and Junnosuke Kobara, "Japan weighs Senkaku options as Chinese coast guard gets new power," *Nikkei Asia*, April 2, 2021, https://asia.nikkei.com/Politics/Japan-weighs-Senkaku-options-as-Chinese-coast-guard-gets-new-power

(2) Taiwan

Around the Taiwan Strait, China's rapid military modernization is changing the strategic balance with Taiwan and provoking Taiwan militarily. Chinese fighter jets have repeatedly entered Taiwan's air space. On April 12, 2021, in one day, 25 Chinese military planes entered Taiwan's Air Identification Zone.[3] And its activities on the Pacific side of Taiwan, where a Chinese aircraft carrier battle group made repeated visits, are of particular concern. If Chinese armed forces deploy there permanently, it would cut Taiwan off from the United States and Japan. Chinese submarine activities are also cause for concern. Given all this, US Indo-Pacific commander Adm. Philip Davidson recently warned that China could invade Taiwan within six years.[4]

In addition, Taiwan is facing diplomatic isolation. Since June 2017, Panama, the Dominican Republic, Burkina Faso, El Salvador, the Solomon Islands, and Kiribati have abandoned formal diplomatic relations with Taiwan as a result of Chinese pressure, including economic assistance and infrastructure projects. This leaves only fifteen countries with formal diplomatic relations with Taiwan. The COVID-19 crisis has made many countries aware that Taiwan cannot join

[3]Brad Lendon, "China sends 25 warplanes into Taiwan's air defense zone, Taipei says," CNN, April 13, 2021, https://edition.cnn.com/2021/04/12/china/china-taiwan-jets-defense-zone-incursion-intl-hnk-ml/index.html

[4]"China could invade Taiwan in next six years, top US admiral warns," *The Guardian*, March 10, 2021, https://www.theguardian.com/world/2021/mar/10/china-could-invade-taiwan-in-next-six-years-top-us-admiral-warns

international organizations like the World Health Organization because of Chinese opposition.

(3) The South China Sea

China has had territorial ambitions in the South China Sea for a long time and has gradually expanded its territories there one by one. China occupied half of the Paracel Islands just after France withdrew from Indochina in the 1950s. It took all of the Paracel Islands just after the US withdrew from Vietnam in the 1970s. China advanced and occupied six features in the Spratly Islands just after the Soviet Union reduced its troops in Vietnam in the 1980s. In the 1990s, China took the Mischief Islands just after the US withdrew from the Philippines.

Recently, China's activities have escalated. While in 2016 the Permanent Court of Arbitration in The Hague rejected China's claim to ownership of 90 percent of the South China Sea, Beijing is ignoring the verdict and building three new airports on seven artificial islands in the South China Sea. And despite China's explanation that these islands will not serve a military purpose, it has started to deploy military planes there.

(4) The Indian Ocean

China has also been active in the Indian Ocean, in three respects. First, China is investing in developing ports such as Gwadar in Pakistan, Hambantota in Sri Lanka, Chittagong in Bangladesh, and Kyaukpyu in Myanmar in the Indian Ocean. Because of the sheer size of China's investments and the 6-8 percent interest rates it charges on loans, these countries now have enormous debts (the World Bank and Asia Development Bank, in contrast, charge 0.25-3 percent).[5] With Hambantota, Sri Lanka was unable to repay its loan. It thus became a victim of China's "debt diplomacy" and in December 2017 handed over the port to China as part of a 99-year lease agreement. Referring to China's development of ports, some raise concern that if the Chinese navy begins to use civil-purpose ports as naval supply bases, China could overcome its strategic weakness, which is its lack of a naval port in the region.

Second, China also exports weapons including submarines to countries around India. Bangladesh received two Chinese submarines in 2016, and Pakistan decided to import eight for its navy. To train the crew and maintain the equipment, Chinese armed forces officers are dispatched to these countries.

And third, China has expanded its military activities in the Indian Ocean since 2009 when it joined anti-piracy exercises off the coast of Somalia. Chinese submarines have patrolled since 2012, and the Chinese surface fleet has called at ports in all the countries around India, including Pakistan, the Maldives, Sri Lanka, Bangladesh, and Myanmar. According to Admiral Sunil Lanba, then-chief of the naval staff of the Indian navy, Beijing has deployed 6-8 warships in

[5]Dipanjan Roy Chaudhury, "China May Put South Asia on Road to Debt Trap," *The Economic Times*, May 2, 2017, http://economictimes.indiatimes.com/news/politics-and-nation/china-may-put-south-asia-on-road-to-debt-trap/articleshow/58467309.cms

the Indian Ocean.[6] In addition, in Pakistan, China has started to deploy ground forces.

Figure 2: China's activities in the Indian Ocean

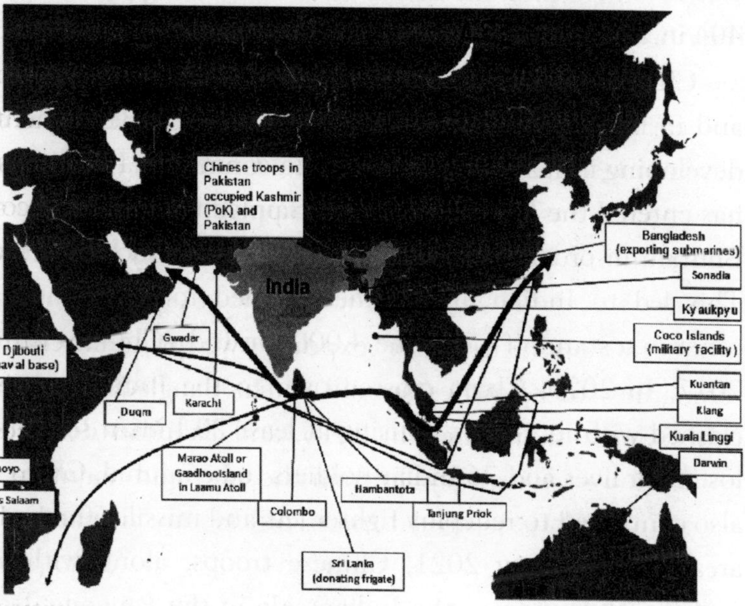

Source: author

(5) The Indo-China border area

Similarly, since 2000 China has been developing infrastructure projects in the Indo-China border area and increasing the number of strategic roads, trains, tunnels, bridges, and airports. Along with these infrastructure projects, China has been increasing troops in the border area and its

[6] "China's Growing Presence in Indian Ocean Challenge for India: Navy Chief," NDTV, March 14, 2019, https://www.ndtv.com/india-news/chinas-growing-presence-in-indian-ocean-challenge-for-india-navy-chief-2007615

incursions have multiplied. In 2011, India recorded 213 incursions in the Indo-China border area, but in the following years, the numbers were larger: 426 in 2012, 411 in 2013, 460 in 2014, 428 in 2015, 296 in 2016, and 473 in 2017, 404 in 2018, and 663 in 2019.

China is deploying troops in Pakistan-occupied Kashmir and in the China-Pakistan economic corridor. Beijing is also developing infrastructure projects to connect to Nepal, and it has entered the Doklam Heights, claimed by both China and Bhutan, in order to build a new road to deploy more forces. This led to Indian and Chinese armed forces facing each other in a standoff along the 4,000 km Indo-China border in 2017. In 2020, China crossed over to the Indian side and clashed with its troops, causing at least 20 Indian soldiers to lose their lives and 76 Indian soldiers to be injured. China has also continued to redeploy fighter jets and missiles from other areas. In February 2021, Chinese troops, along with 200 tanks, withdrew from the Indian side in the Pangong Tso in Ladakh, but they have continued to stay on the Indian side in at least four other locations.[7] China is also building villages along the Indo-China border,[8] causing concern that it will treat these villages as military camps.

[7]"India closely watching Chinese air defence batteries deployed near LAC," *The Economic Times*, April 12, 2021, https://economictimes.indiatimes.com/news/defence/india-closely-watching-chinese-air-defence-batteries-deployed-near-lac/articleshow/82032998.cms?utm_source=newsletter&utm_medium=email&utm_campaign=defencenewsletter&ncode=cbbfb77de0d1419d84bc91812de06420

[8]Vishnu Som, "Exclusive: China Has Built Village In Arunachal, Show Satellite Images," NDTV, January 18, 2021, https://www.ndtv.com/india-news/china-has-built-village-in-arunachal-pradesh-show-satellite-images-exclusive-2354154

II. WHAT ARE CHINA'S OBJECTIVES AND WHAT CAN IT ACHIEVE WITH THESE ACTIVITIES?

China is provoking many of its neighbors at the same time, and from a national security standpoint, there are three things China can achieve by doing this:

(1) Defend the coastal cities

It is worth asking why China wants to build seven artificial islands with three runways in the South China Sea and militarize these islands. Former Japanese Prime Minister Shinzo Abe made an interesting observation in a 2012 article: "The South China Sea seems set to become a 'Lake Beijing,' which analysts say will be to China what the Sea of Okhotsk was to Soviet Russia: a sea deep enough for the People's Liberation Army's navy to base their nuclear-powered attack submarines, capable of launching missiles with nuclear warheads."[9] If China deploys nuclear-armed submarines in the South China Sea, the US must take great care to avoid a worst-case scenario. If the US were to attack Chinese facilities there, there is a real possibility that it could escalate into a nuclear war. With the situation so combustible, no one can afford to take risks in the South China Sea.

However, it would be sensible to station American submarines alongside Chinese submarines so that they are able to come by and say "hello." If China wants to establish a deterrent, it will need to ensure that its submarines are not

[9]Shinzo Abe, "Asia's Democratic Security Diamond," *Project Syndicate*, December 27, 2012, https://www.project-syndicate.org/onpoint/a-strategic-alliance-for-japan-and-india-by-shinzo-abe?barrier=accesspaylog

detectable by any foreign ships, planes, or sensors (Figure 3). Therefore, China will need to prevent all foreign vessels that can detect Chinese submarines from entering its zone of influence in the South China Sea. Its goal is to use the artificial islands to form a sacred triangle that can harbor nuclear-armed submarines to deploy missiles, bombers, and fighter jets, and exclude any foreign ships and planes that can detect these submarines. However, China has not yet finished the triangle because it has not built artificial islands in the Scarborough Shoal.

Figure 3. China built artificial islands to create a sacred triangle for nuclear-armed submarines.

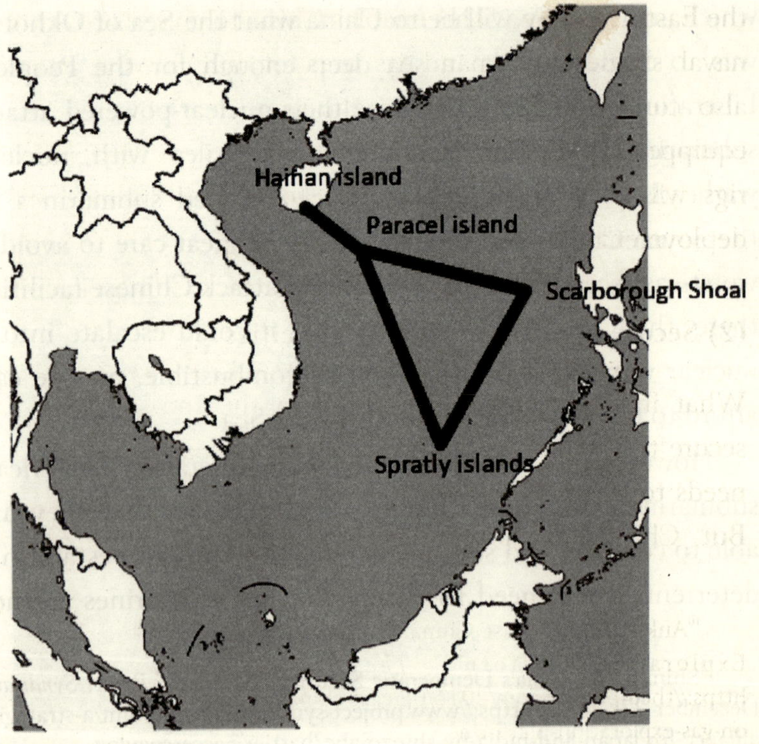

But why does China want to turn the South China Sea into a "fortress," as PM Abe put it? China has spent too much money building these artificial islands for the rationale to be merely economic, so there must also be a security rationale. It is true that China can use its presence in the South China Sea to defend its coastline, and there is good reason for it to do that: many cities and industrial areas along China's coastline are critical for China's overall economic development. One could imagine that China's activities in the South China Sea are like a new type of "Great Wall." But by that same logic, China would also construct similar fortresses in the sea around Japan and Taiwan. In November 2013, China set up a new Air Defense Identification Zone in the East China Sea. This enables China to give air cover to its naval ships and expand its area of influence. China has also constructed oil rigs in the area, many of which are equipped with radar. Japanese experts believe that these oil rigs will play a supporting role to Chinese naval and air deployment.[10]

(2) Secure SLOCs for the coastal cities

What interests does China have in the Indian Ocean? To secure the economic development of its coastal cities, China needs to safeguard its sea lines of communications (SLOCs). But China's economic development depends on SLOCs

[10]Ankit Panda, "East China Sea: Japan Spots Chinese Radar on Gas Exploration Platform," *The Diplomat*, August 9, 2016, https://thediplomat.com/2016/08/east-china-sea-japan-spots-chinese-radar-on-gas-exploration-platform/

through the Malacca Strait, which the US Navy controls, and Chinese economic development would come to a halt if the United States blockaded the strait. To solve this problem, China has created new energy and trade routes: Middle East-Pakistan-China (Xinjiang Uygur), Middle East-Myanmar-China, and others. Nevertheless, Beijing still has cause for worry about its security needs in the Indian Ocean.

To secure its SLOCs, China could deploy its military forces, but without bases it cannot easily do this. That is why China's port development projects have created concern in this region. If the Chinese navy begins to use these civil-purpose ports as naval supply bases to maintain its ships and crew readiness, China could overcome its strategic weakness. Beijing has already established a huge naval base in Djibouti and deployed its warships and marines to the base.[11]

However, China's deployment of submarines or naval ships in the Indian Ocean raises security concerns for other countries. First, Chinese warships can attack the SLOCs of other countries. Second, a strong naval presence could make China a leading security provider in the Indian Ocean. Historically, the main security providers in the Indian Ocean have been the US and India, and China's activities are now escalating competition between them. And third, Chinese submarines could potentially attack India's nuclear ballistic-missile submarines, compromising India's nuclear deterrence

[11]Ryan Pickrell, "China's overseas naval base is now big enough for its aircraft carriers, a top US commander says", Business Insider, Apr 22, 2021, https://www.businessinsider.com/chinas-overseas-base-big-enough-for-aircraft-carriers-us-commander-2021-4

against China. The presence of Chinese submarines also forces India to restrain its deployment of aircraft carriers.

(3) Obtain natural resources for coastal cities

The Indo-China border is nearly uninhabitable because of its high altitude, harsh terrain, and extreme climate. Despite such conditions, China has expanded its territories there. There is a strong possibility that China's interest in this area is related to its interests in its coastal cities. China's military provocations have escalated since it started developing infrastructure in Tibet and the Xinjiang Uygur region around 2000. The reason China started to develop these inland areas is because its coastal cities need more natural resources including water, minerals, and agriculture products. The Tibet region is rich in water resources and is the riverhead of many rivers including the Indus River, the Ganges River, the Brahmaputra River, the Mekong River, the Yangtze River and the Yellow River. As a result, China is building many dams and diverting water from Tibet, which may prevent countries downstream from getting enough water resources in the near future. Indeed, some media reports claim that China is planning to divert water from Tibet to Xinjiang to change the desert areas into fertile agricultural land.[12] In addition, despite Tibet's rich mineral resources, the limitations of its terrain have restricted development of these resources for a

[12]Stephen Chen, "Chinese engineers plan 1,000km tunnel to make Xinjiang desert bloom," *South China Morning Post*, October 29, 2021, https://www.scmp.com/news/china/society/article/2116750/chinese-engineers-plan-1000km-tunnel-make-xinjiang-desert-bloom

long time. The main consumers of water, agricultural products, mineral resources live in cities along the coastline.

In addition, the land routes along Tibet and Xinjiang Uygur are important to China for trade and for importing energy resources from the Middle East. For example, if China imports oil from the Middle East through the Indian Ocean and Pakistan, the oil goes through Pakistan-occupied Kashmir. Xinjiang Uygur or Tibet provide alternatives to reaching China's coastal cities. The Ladakh region of India is located along the route. Any military efforts in Ladakh could pose a threat to China, so it is trying to stop India's efforts to defend its border in Ladakh.

III. CONCLUSION: HOW TO DEAL WITH CHINA

Why has China escalated its military activities? The reason is related to the economic development of coastal cities in China. China has tried to exclude foreign militaries as far as possible from these cities, safeguard its SLOCs leading to the cities, and ensure enough water and other natural resources reach the cities.

Defending itself is not wrong. But China has not respected the interests of other countries, and that is cause for concern. Along with its military modernization, China's provocative attitude has escalated. Therefore, countries that suffer as a result of China's assertiveness should collaborate and demand China follow current international rules and respect their interests in a multinational framework. At the same time, the countries around China must build up their military power to contain China's assertiveness. That is why cooperation in the Indo-Pacific, through the QUAD+ framework (India-US-Japan-Australia, along with other countries), is very important.

(Dr Satoru Nagao, a prominent scholar on Indo-Pacific region, is associated with the US-based Hudson Institute)

Chapter 2

Maintaining Regional Influence: Australia's Response to China's South Pacific Challenge

– Grant Wyeth

In April 2020, a Royal Australian Air Force (RAAF) transport aircraft was attempting to land at Vanuatu's Port Vila airport. The aircraft was scheduled to deliver supplies to the Melanesian country after the devastating effects of Cyclone Harold. However, the pilot was unable to land. Parked on the runway was another aircraft, one that had been chartered by the China Civil Engineering Construction Corporation (CCECC). Without the space to land safely, and lacking the fuel to continue circling for an unknown time period, the RAAF aircraft was forced to return to Brisbane.[1]

The supplies were delivered the following day, causing only minimal disruption, but the event was highly symbolic. It was a signal of China's growing presence in the South Pacific, and the challenge that Australia now faces to maintain its influence in the region.

[1]Anthony Galloway, Defence Looks at Chinese Plane Blocking Australian Plane in Vanuatu, Sydney Morning Herald, 15 April, 2020. https://www.smh.com.au/politics/federal/defence-looks-at-chinese-plane-blocking-australian-aid-plane-in-vanuatu-20200415-p54k5i.html

Australia's primary security objective is to prevent any unaligned powers from gaining military access to the Pacific Islands. The strategy is built on the fear that were this presence to be established it could be used as either a forward-base for an assault on Australia itself, or limit Australia's ability to maneuver throughout the South Pacific.[2]

This concern has extended as far back as the late 1800s - prior to the formulation of the modern Australian state - with the local suspicion of German activity in New Guinea and Bougainville. The then-separate colonies on the Australian continent urged the British government to annex these territories in order to prevent a German foothold.[3] The British made some efforts to honour this request - seizing the south-eastern portion of the island of New Guinea - but it wasn't until the outbreak of World War I that the German presence was eradicated. With Australian troops themselves fully capturing German protectorates in the region, and subsequently governing these as external territories until 1975.

Japanese expansion into the South Pacific in the early-1940s proposed the next problem for Australia.

The Japanese strategy of attempting to isolate Australia from its ally in the United States by advancing through South-East Asia and the South Pacific confirmed Australia's anxiety about its own geographic dilemma. The bombing of Darwin heightened fears of a Japanese invasion, although this was

[2]Sam Bateman and Anthony Bergin, Staying the Course: Australia and maritime security in the South Pacific, Analysis and Policy Observatory, 2 June 2011. https://apo.org.au/node/25024

[3]C Hartley Grattan, Australia and the Pacific, Foreign Affairs, October 1928. https://www.foreignaffairs.com/articles/australia/1928-10-01/australia-and-pacific

never a serious consideration of Japan's expansionist plans, given the man-power it would take to hold such a large landmass.[4]

However, the defeat and realignment of the Japanese as a Western ally – and now one of Australia's closest security partners – enabled Australia to consolidate the South Pacific as its zone of influence. Working in tandem with its cousins in New Zealand, Canberra had until recently been able to establish a comfortable hegemony in the region.[5] With Australia focusing its attention on the Melanesia sub-region, and New Zealand focusing on Polynesia. Although with considerable overlap.

The establishment of the Pacific Island Forum (PIF) in 1971 created a multilateral framework for Australia and New Zealand to cooperate with the states of Melanesia, Polynesia, and Micronesia in areas of economic interest, maritime security, and the ever-present natural disaster relief. This body gave Pacific Island countries a far greater opportunity to have their concerns identified and understood by its larger and more powerful neighbours. But it also kept these countries close to Australia's own strategic interests.

Yet the rapid rise of China as a global power has disrupted this comfortable arrangement by establishing a new powerful non-aligned presence in the Pacific. China has now become the

[4]Gary Brown and David Anderson, Invasion 1942? Australia and the Japanese Threat, Background Paper Number 6 1992, Department of the Parliamentary Library, Canberra. 29 April 1992. https://www.aph.gov.au/binaries/library/pubs/bp/1992/92bp06.pdf

[5]Jonathan Pryke, The Risks of China's Ambitions in the South Pacific, Brookings Institute, 20 July 2020. https://www.brookings.edu/articles/the-risks-of-chinas-ambitions-in-the-south-pacific/

largest trading partner for many Pacific Island countries, and is second only to Australia in both investment and aid.[6] This has spooked the Australian government who are wary of not only China's burgeoning influence, but the way Beijing uses its economic muscle to coerce countries.

Initially China's primary interest in the region was to pick off the last remaining diplomatic allies that Taiwan had in the Pacific. The ethnic and cultural links between Micronesia and Taiwan's indigenous population had enabled Taipei to maintain a strong diplomatic recognition throughout the Pacific even as the global tide of establishing formal links with the People's Republic of China accelerated in the 1970s.[7]

During the Taiwanese Presidency of Ma Ying-jeou (2008-2016) a tacit agreement was reached between Beijing and Taipei to maintain the status quo and cease competition for diplomatic recognition.[8] However, since the election of President Tsai Ing-wen in 2016, Beijing has increased its pressure on Pacific Island states to end their recognition of Taiwan. In late-2019, both the Solomon Islands and Kiribati

[6]Ethan Meick et al, China's Engagement in the Pacific Islands Implications for the United States, staff research report, US–China Economic and Security Review Commission, 14 June 2018. https://www.uscc.gov/sites/default/files/Research/China-Pacific%20Islands%20Staff%20Report.pdf

[7]Grant Wyeth,, Taiwan and the Pacific: One Big, Happy Austronesian Family, The Diplomat, 9 January, 2019. https://thediplomat.com/2019/01/taiwan-and-the-pacific-one-big-happy-austronesian-family/

[8]Dean Chen, The Strategic Implications of Ma Ying-jeou's "One ROC, Two Areas" Policy on Cross-Strait Relations, American Journal of Chinese Studies, pp 23-41, Vol, 20, No1. 2013 www.jstor.org/stable/44289005

succumbed to this pressure and established formal diplomatic ties with Beijing.[9,10]

This leaves only three Micronesian states of Marshall Islands, Nauru, Pulau, and the Polynesian country of Tuvalu, maintaining their diplomatic recognition of Taiwan.

These diplomatic shifts have been driven mostly by economic realities. The Solomon Islands' lush rainforests have proved a major source of wood for China in the past two decades, with 90% of the country's logging exports now going to China.[11] However, the economic benefits of this have accrued mostly to elite and state actors, creating tensions with local villages who have seen their natural habitats destroyed, as well as conflict between provinces and the central government.[12, 13] But the size of the industry and its influence on the central government made resisting Beijing's demands for recognition impossible.

[9]David Crawshaw et al, China Intensifies Pacific Offensive as Taiwan Loses Another Ally, The Washington Post, 20 September 2019. https://www.washingtonpost.com/world/asia_pacific/chinas-pacific-offensive-intensifies-as-taiwan-cuts-relations-with-kiribati/2019/09/20/bccd26d8-db69-11e9-a1a5-162b8a9c9ca2_story.html

[10]Edward Cavanough, When China Came Calling: Inside the Solomon Islands Switch, The Guardian, 7 December 2019. https://www.theguardian.com/world/2019/dec/08/when-china-came-calling-inside-the-solomon-islands-switch

[11]Josh Nichols, The $3bn Bargain: How China Dominates Pacific Mining, Logging, and Fishing, The Guardian, 30 May, 2021. https://www.theguardian.com/world/2021/may/31/the-3bn-bargain-how-china-dominates-pacific-mining-logging-and-fishing

[12]John Beck,, Logging is Corrupting these Islands: One Village Fights Back – and Wins, National Geographic, 4 January 2020. https://www.nationalgeographic.com/science/article/deforestation-in-the-solomon-islands

[13]Edward Cavanough, Solomon Islands Province Announces Independence Vote Amid China Tensions, The Guardian, 2 September 2020. https://www.theguardian.com/world/2020/sep/02/solomon-islands-province-announces-independence-vote-amid-china-tensions

Just over half the seafood, wood, and mineral resources exported from the Pacific Islands now goes to China. The total of China's consumption of these resources was greater than the next 10 Pacific trading partners combined.[14] Giving an indication of the economic weight that Beijing has rapidly acquired in the Pacific, and the obvious influence that stems from this economic activity.

It is these harder forms of power that are driving China's engagement in the Pacific. Beijing struggles with an instinctive understanding of what soft power entails. The general ideals, ways of thinking, and habits of attraction and cooperation are not natural to authoritarian regimes, who don't inhabit these modes of behaviour at home, and therefore cannot fully embody them abroad.[15] So while Beijing has been able to forge elite-level contacts throughout the region, and use these relationships to establish a presence through trade relations, political favours, and the provision of aid projects, they still have yet to gain public trust.

In the April 2020 elections in Samoa, one of the key issues was a decision by the previous government to award a contract to a Chinese state-owned enterprise for the building of a new port, to be funded by a loan from Beijing. The opposition campaigned on cancelling the project and successfully won the

[14]Josh Nichols, The $3bn Bargain: How China Dominates Pacific Mining, Logging, and Fishing, The Guardian, 30 May, 2021. https://www.theguardian.com/world/2021/may/31/the-3bn-bargain-how-china-dominates-pacific-mining-logging-and-fishing

[15]David Shambaugh, China's Soft-Power Push, Foreign Affairs, July/August 2015. https://www.foreignaffairs.com/articles/china/2015-06-16/chinas-soft-power-push

election, demonstrating that Pacific public are well-attuned to China's growing influence and hold reservations towards it.[16]

However, China has created a narrative that does attempt to speak to the histories of Pacific Island countries and their places in the world. Despite its growing wealth and power, China has portrayed itself to the Pacific as a fellow-developing country, one who can empathise with their colonial experiences, and can offer a new path towards their own development that doesn't come via the traditional European and North American powers, or indeed Australia and New Zealand.[17]

Yet this approach relies on an expected lack of sophistication among Pacific Islanders. Hoping that they won't have a strong understanding of the Chinese Communist Party's ideology and mode of operations. Contrary to this hope in Beijing, Pacific Islands have instead proved themselves reasonably adept at leveraging their sovereignty for gains within the international system.[18] An emerging power like China offers Pacific Islands opportunities, but opportunities that can be balanced against traditional relationships in order to facilitate local requirements.

Pacific Island states have unique needs that countries with continuous land masses do not. Dispersed groups of islands

[16]Jonathan Barrett, Samoa to Scrap China-backed Port Project Under New Leader, Reuters, 20 May, 2021. https://www.reuters.com/world/asia-pacific/samoa-shelve-china-backed-port-project-under-new-leader-2021-05-20/

[17]Richard Herr, Chinese Influence in the Pacific Islands, Australian Strategic Policy Institute, 30 April 2019. https://www.aspi.org.au/report/chinese-influence-pacific-islands

[18]Lizzie Yarina, "Micro-statecraft: Sovereignty as Currency for Oceania's Island States." Informa, Issue 12: pp 216–231. 2019. https://revistas.upr.edu/images/informa/2020/v12/art4.pdf

make service delivery both difficult and expensive. A lack of high valued-added resources means that the ability to harness domestic revenues to deliver these resources is limited. The persistent exposure to natural disasters also creates a hindrance on economic development. Australia has seen that its strategic concerns require taking considerable responsibility for these inherent difficulties.

Yet reliance on Australia, and its close partner New Zealand, can be deemed limiting by Pacific Island countries. Particularly when Canberra and Wellington have tied their assistance to the maintenance of Western democratic institutions. This is something that Fijian Prime Minister, Frank Bainimarama has especially bristled at, having initially come to power via a military coup, and who subsequently found himself ostracised by Australia and New Zealand, leading to Fiji being suspended from the Pacific Islands Forum from 2009 to 2014.

Bainimarama's reaction to this was a new "Look North" foreign policy that sought to circumvent Fiji's traditional partners. Being unconcerned with how Bainmarama came to power, or the health of Fiji's institutions, Beijing sensed an opportunity to enhance its presence in the Pacific. Following Bainimarama's coup China's development aid to Fiji increased by sevenfold, with Bainimarama responding by stating that "the Government of the People's Republic of China expressed confidence in our ability to resolve our problems in our way, without undue pressure of interference." A none-too-subtle reference to Australia.[19]

[19]Jian Yang, China in Fiji: Displacing Traditional Players?, The Pacific Islands in China's Grand Strategy. Palgrave Macmillan, New York. 2011. https://doi.org/10.1057/9780230339750_6

While these increases in aid still fell well short of the assistance that Australia provides to the region, it is the type of aid that creates the attention. China tends to focus on large infrastructure projects that will create significant public exposure, like sport stadiums and airport expansions.[20] These projects are also delivered by Chinese state-owned enterprises like the China Civil Engineering Construction Corporation, providing these companies with a foothold in Pacific Islands.[21] But many of these projects are also delivered as loans, which creates considerable concern in Canberra over whether repayments are able to be met by Pacific governments, and what will be China's response if they are not met.[22]

A replication of the situation with Sri Lanka's Hambantota Port - where the port was leased to China for 99 years due to Colombo's inability to repay their debts to Beijing – is something Australia is keen to avoid.[23] There have been rumours China's construction of a wharf in Vanuatu would be converted into a naval base, and also that Beijing was set to lease an entire island in the Solomon Islands, but neither of these rumours have been substantiated. However, the ongoing fear in Canberra is that China will eventually use the leverage it

[20]Merriden Varrall, Understanding China's Approach to Aid, The Lowy Interpreter, 12 January 2018. https://www.lowyinstitute.org/the-interpreter/understanding-chinas-approach-aid

[21]Jonathan Pryke, The Risks of China's Ambitions in the South Pacific, Brookings Institute, 20 July 2020. https://www.brookings.edu/articles/the-risks-of-chinas-ambitions-in-the-south-pacific/

[22]Merriden Varrall, Understanding China's Approach to Aid, The Lowy Interpreter, 12 January 2018. https://www.lowyinstitute.org/the-interpreter/understanding-chinas-approach-aid

[23]Maria Abi-Habib, How China Got Sri Lanka to Cough up a Port, New York Times, 25 June 2018. https://www.nytimes.com/2018/06/25/world/asia/china-sri-lanka-port.html

has gained through diplomacy, trade, infrastructure, cheap loans, and the capture of local elites to gain some form of military access to one or more Pacific Islands.

This concern is grounded in the "island chain" thesis within China's strategic thinking. Although initially conceived by American military planners as a framework for limiting the maritime maneuvers in the Pacific of the Soviet Union and subsequently the People's Republic of China, it has come to be adopted by Beijing as its own framework for freeing itself of these constraints, and in particular limiting the ability of other states to defend Taiwan.[24,25]

Through this maritime framework the first island chain runs from the Japanese islands in the East China Sea, through Taiwan, and the Philippines into the South China Sea. The second island chain runs through Micronesia - with its significant U.S presence - to the island of New Guinea. With the third running from the Aleutian Islands, through Hawaii, and into the central Pacific crossover from Melanesia to Polynesia.

Although China currently lacks the capabilities to fully secure even the first island chain, should the United States retrench from its Western Pacific commitments, the balance of power in the region would tip considerably in Beijing's favour. Australia and other regional middle powers like Japan would lack the ability to constrain China by themselves, and the

[24]Wilson Vorndick, China's Reach Has Grown, So Should the Island Chains, Asia Maritime Transparency Initiative, 22 October, 2018. https://amti.csis.org/chinas-reach-grown-island-chains/

[25]Toshi Yoshihara, China's Vision of its Seascape: The First Island China and Chinese Seapower, APP Asian Politics and Policy, 5 July 2012. https://onlinelibrary.wiley.com/doi/abs/10.1111/j.1943-0787.2012.01349.x

Pacific Island states in the third island chain would then become much more vulnerable to Chinese designs.

However, concerns both in Canberra and in Washington over China's rapidly increasing maritime capabilities are pronounced enough for new military investments to be made. Most notably has been the upgrading of the Lombrum Naval Base on Manus Island, off the north coast of Papua New Guinea, as a joint Australia-US-Papua New Guinea venture. Manus Island is a key strategic location that provides excellent maritime access into the wider Pacific, as well as the ability to launch vessels towards northeast Asia and crucially, the South China Sea.[26]

The upgrading of the Lombrum Naval Base forms an essential component of Australia's broader "Pacific Step-Up". This has been the overarching label for Australia making a noticeable re-engagement in the Pacific in the face of China's increased presence. This has included a substantial increase in development assistance, as well as the creation of the Australian Infrastructure Financing Facility for the Pacific, which will provide both grants and loans to fund essential energy, water, transport and telecommunications infrastructure for Pacific Island countries (and Timor Leste).[27]

One notable project falling under this umbrella is the Coral Sea Cable System, which will link high speed fibre optic cable

[26]Natalie Whiting, Joint US-Australian Naval Base on Manus Island a 'Significant Pushback' against China's Pacific Ambitions, Australian Broadcasting Corporation, 18 November 2018 https://www.abc.net.au/news/2018-11-18/us-pushes-further-into-pacific-with-png-manus-naval-base-deal/10508354

[27]Merriden Varrall, Australia's Response to China in the Pacific: From Alert to Alarmed, In: The China Alternative: Changing Regional Order in the Pacific Islands, ed: edited by Graeme Smith and Terence Wesley-Smith, pp 107-42. ANU Press, 2021. https://www.jstor.org/stable/j.ctv1h45mkn.7

from Sydney to both Honiara in the Solomon Islands and Port Moresby in Papua New Guinea. This project was a direct response to an agreement the Solomon Islands were negotiating with Huawei. Australian security agencies warned of the risks associated with Huawei's intimate relationship with the Chinese Communist Party, and so the Australian government stepped in to outbid the Chinese firm. Expanding the project to include Port Moresby.[28]

Essential to Australia's Pacific Step-Up has been realigned Bainimarama back towards Canberra. Bainimarma's "Look North" policy had not only brought a greater Chinese presence in the Pacific, but had also enabled the Fijian prime minister to establish himself as the central political actor through the Pacific Islands, unrestrained by the conventions of Pacific Island Forum.[29] Bainimarama had also become the drive-force behind the collective attempt of Pacific Island countries to reframe themselves as "large ocean states", rather than "small island countries".[30] Placing environmental issues at the centre of their diplomatic efforts, and seeking new partnerships that understood the Pacific's unique.

In 2019, Australia Prime Minister, Scott Morrison, made two trips to Suva to establish a rapport with the Fijian leader.

[28]Patrick Begley, Sea Cable Boosts ties to PNG, Solomon Islands amid China influence, Sydney Morning Herald, 28 August 2019. https://www.smh.com.au/world/asia/sea-cable-boosts-ties-to-png-solomon-islands-amid-china-influence-20190828-p52lpt.html

[29]Grant Wyeth and Larissa Stünkel, Fiji First, then the World, Foreign Policy, 15 February 2021. https://foreignpolicy.com/2021/02/15/first-fiji-then-the-world/

[30]Grant Wyeth, Paying Attention to the Blue Pacific, The Diplomat, 30 October, 2018. https://thediplomat.com/2018/10/paying-attention-to-the-blue-pacific/

The two bonded over their love of rugby and Christian faith, and laid the groundwork for a new comprehensive strategic partnership between the two countries. This would be known as the Fiji-Australia Vuvale Partnership (vuvale meaning family in the iTaukei language). The concept being that families can have disputes, but they are bonded by connections that transcend any occasional disagreements.[31]

Later in 2019 Bainimarama made the trip to Canberra to sign the agreement, where he was afforded a ceremonial welcome, with a military guard of honour, signalling his transformation from pariah to fêted leader. It was a demonstration that he had played the new geopolitical conditions in the Pacific to his advantage. Understanding that Australia's fears about China would eventually lead Canberra to overlook the way he initially came to power, and instead take a more realist approach to the region's political landscape.

The shifting geopolitical landscape has provided Pacific Island leaders with greater leverage to gain Australia's attention. It must be noted that these countries do have an awareness of the risks associated with engagement with the Chinese Communist Party, and they maintain a strong preference for their traditional partners in Australia and New Zealand. Beijing has considerable cultural constraints in the Pacific, which instead favour Canberra and Wellington.[32]

[31]Grant Wyeth and Larissa Stünkel, Fiji First, then the World, Foreign Policy, 15 February 2021. https://foreignpolicy.com/2021/02/15/first-fiji-then-the-world/

[32]Denghua Zhang, China constrained as much as controlling in the South Pacific, East Asia Forum, 16 May, 2019. https://www.eastasiaforum.org/2019/05/16/china-constrained-as-much-as-controlling-in-the-south-pacific/

However, Canberra's inability to take the Pacific's primary security threat – climate change – seriously remains a source of continued frustration.

The transnational nature of Climate Change is something that is keenly felt in the Pacific. These are countries that emit negligible amounts of carbon themselves, but disproportionately experience the effects of major weather events, and rising sea levels. Countries whose land masses only barely rise above sea level, like Tuvalu, Kiribati, and Nauru, see the impacts of Climate Change in very real, existential terms.[33]

Here Australia's foreign policy objectives are being hampered by its domestic politics. A faction within Australia conservative coalition government that simply refuses to accept the reality of man-made climate change prevents the country from being able to phase out its reliance on coal-fired energy consumption. As well as Australia's substantial coal export industry.[34] Domestic political calculations also play their part, with federal elections in Australia being effectively won in Queensland and in particular in seats where coal mining is a major local employer.[35]

[33]Richard Curtain and Matthew Dornan, Climate change and migration in Kiribati, Tuvalu and Nauru, Development Policy Centre, 15 February 2019. https://devpolicy.org/climate-change-migration-kiribati-tuvalu-nauru-20190215/

[34]Grant Wyeth, Australia Domestic Politics Hamstrings its Pacific Foreign Policy, The Diplomat, 10 September, 2018. https://thediplomat.com/2018/09/australias-domestic-politics-hamstrings-its-pacific-foreign-policy/

[35]Allyson Horn, Election 2019: Why Queensland Turned its Back on Labor and Helped Scott Morrision to Victory, Australian Broadcasting Corporation, 19 May 2019. https://www.abc.net.au/news/2019-05-19/election-results-how-labor-lost-queensland/11122998

Because of this the Australian government is proving incapable of forming any kind of carbon reduction policy that could send a reassuring signal to its Pacific neighbours. Bainimarama had even suggested that the reason Pacific Island countries were turning to Beijing was due Australia's recalcitrance towards action on Climate Change.[36] Although China produces and uses far more coal than Australia, it was another attempt by Bainimarama to leverage Beijing's presence for the Pacific's goals in relation to Canberra.

China's rise has provided Pacific Island countries with a tool to ask Australia to give their concerns greater consideration. These states know that they need Australia in order to help them advance their interests in the international community. They simply don't have the weight to do so by themselves, requiring their local regional power to often act as their champion.

Pacific Island countries are also aware that any major changes to the current geopolitical order from a revisionist China could prove far more disadvantageous to them. This make Pacific Island countries keen multilateralists. They understand that a world where superpowers do not submit themselves to an agreed upon set of rules, and believe that they are above international institutions that seek to provide avenues for smaller states to have their concerns considered would create further burdens for them.[37]

[36]Kate Lyons, Fiji PM accuses Scott Morrison of 'insulting' and alienating Pacific leaders, The Guardian, 17 August 2019. https://www.theguardian.com/world/2019/aug/16/fiji-pm-frank-bainimarama-insulting-scott-morrison-rift-pacific-countries

[37]Lizzie Yarina, "Micro-statecraft: Sovereignty as Currency for Oceania's Island States." Informa, Issue 12: pp 216–231. 2019. https://revistas.upr.edu/images/informa/2020/v12/art4.pdf

These perspectives align with Australia's own strategic interests to prevent unaligned powers from gaining a foothold in the Pacific Islands. While the influence of China's market and its desire to influence other states regardless of their size is not to be discounted, Australia also maintains a significant advantage in people-to-people links, with its strong cultural, political and social bonds, including significant Pacific diasporas.[38]

This advantage most notably expands to Australia's ability to provide labour mobility for Pacific Islanders, something Beijing cannot match. There is a correlation between Australia's continual need for agricultural labour, and Pacific Islanders' desire to earn wages in high income countries. The creation of the Seasonal Workers Programme and the Pacific Labour Scheme by Canberra has aimed to service this correlation of needs. Pacific Island leaders are keen to expand these programmes, seeing the tangible benefits in both remittances and skill-development that are returned to their countries.[39]

Australia's growing concern about China's increased presence in the Pacific is based on the belief that the Chinese Communist Party's intent of rewriting the rules of the global order to undermine its mutually beneficial ideals, to establish a

[38]James Batley, What Does the 2016 Census Reveal about Pacific Islands Communities in Australia?, State, Society and Governance in Melanesia, ANU College of Asia & the Pacific, September 2017. http://bellschool.anu.edu.au/sites/default/files/publications/attachments/2017-09/ib_2017_23_batley_revised_final_0.pdf

[39]Stephen Howes, Time for a Permanent Australian Step-Up in Pacific Labour Mobility, Development Policy Centre, 12 December 2019. https://devpolicy.org/time-for-a-permanent-australian-step-up-in-pacific-labour-mobility-20191212/

system that is more submissive to China's desires and sensitivities. Due to this, Canberra remains concerned not just about the strategic intent of China's activity in the South Pacific, but also the effectiveness of its developmental aid, its fostering of local corruption, and its potential to create debt traps that could be used as leverage.[40]

However, Pacific Island countries should be given the respect to make their own evaluations about the opportunities and costs of their relationships with China. Undermining their sovereign rights won't enhance regional trust. Yet Australia clearly sees its own interests in offering better opportunities to Pacific Island countries, and for the most part – Climate Change aside – Pacific Islanders would understand the rewards are greater and the costs minimal to maintaining their close links with their traditional partner in Canberra.

(Grant Wyeth is a columnist for the noted Asia-Pacific affairs publication The Diplomat).

[40]Merriden Varrall, Australia's Response to China in the Pacific: From Alert to Alarmed, In: The China Alternative: Changing Regional Order in the Pacific Islands, ed: edited by Graeme Smith and Terence Wesley-Smith, pp 107-42. ANU Press, 2021. https://www.jstor.org/stable/j.ctv1h45mkn.7

Chapter 3

Why Bangladesh is Important to China

– Mohshin Habib

On 27 April, 2021, Chinese defense minister, who also holds the rank of state councilor, Wei Fenghe abruptly visited Bangladesh and met with President Abdul Hamid and then Chief of Bangladesh Army Staff General Aziz Ahmed. He also paid homage to the Father of the Nation Bangabandhu Sheikh Mujibur Rahman at Bangabandhu Memorial Museum at Dhanmondi 32, where the leader was killed along with almost all of his family members in 1975—China, like Pakistan, recognized Bangladesh after the infamous assassination of Bangabandhu Sheikh Mujib. It should also be noted that Sheikh Mujibur Rahman left behind two daughters, who, at the time of the killing, were visiting Germany. The elder Daughter of him, Sheikh Hasina, is now the Prime Minister of Bangladesh.

The day Wei visited Bangladesh was not a perfect day for the host country as it saw 97 deaths and more than 3000 new Corona cases—and an increasingly tightened lock dawn was going on. During such a situation, no country receives any guest and neither sends any delegate abroad. So, for the people of Bangladesh Wei was nothing but a gatecrasher. At that time people were told that the purpose of his visit was discussing covid-19 and bilateral military cooperation. As he called on Bangladeshi President, he remarked that China and Bangladesh should make joint efforts against powers from outside the region establishing a military alliance in South Asia and practicing hegemony. He did not formally mentioned any power's name. Bangladeshis have taken this statement as a formal one.

Usually when a diplomat or a leader visits another country, they speak in that way. Therefore, the people of Bangladesh did not buy Wei's statement. They believed that China has a secret agenda. Noticeably, in November 2020, Wei was scheduled to visit Bangladesh after finishing his Nepal visit. But his Bangladesh visit at that time was cancelled at the last moment. Although Wei claimed that the time was not suitable enough to visit Bangladesh, there was no official explanation cited by any side about the cancelation.

In last November, the pandemic situation in Bangladesh had been much better than that of 27 April, 2021, the day Wei visited Bangladesh. That is why his visit to Bangladesh, to some Bangladeshis, was unusual and there is a perception that China had something to say, which could have been heard by a few diplomats and policymakers of both sides.

Chinese officials, however, did not take too much time to outline their intentions. Later, on May 10, Chinese Ambassador to Bangladesh Li Jiming said that the relations between Bangladesh and China will be substantially get damaged if the country join Quad. His statement was not only aggressive, it was also violation of diplomatic norms and humiliation of a country's sovereignty.

Now people of Bangladesh are convinced that Quad issue

was one of the main purposes of Wei's visit and it was a clear threat to Bangladesh.

Now the questions can be asked: What is Quad? Is there any chance for Bangladesh to join it? If not, then why Bangladesh is being threatened by the Asian giant? Why China considers Bangladesh so important for Indo-Pacific power politics?

Quadrilateral Security Dialogue, well known as Quad, is a dialogue initiated in 2007 by the then Japanese Prime Minister Shinzo Abe with the support of then Indian Prime Minister Manmohan Singh, Australian Prime Minister John Howard and then US Vice President Dick Cheney. Simultaneously the countries placed a joint military exercise titled Exercise Malabar. The first naval exercise named Malabar-1 held in 1992 between India and United States.

Perhaps Quad is expanding, yes. In March 2020, the quad key member countries held a meeting of the Quad Plus on Covid-19 pandemic where New Zealand, South Korea and Vietnam was approached. On 12 March 2021, a Quad summit was held virtually. It was reported before the summit that the four member countries are working to develop a plan to distribute Covid-19 vaccines to the Asian countries as part of a broader strategy to counter China's influence.

Whatever the policy, China is robustly considering this alliance as Asian NATO, that is being created to thwarting China's economical and military influence. So, Beijing has become more aggressive toward India-Bangladesh relations.

But Bangladesh, an economically weak but important in geo-political strategy, situated at the navel point of India, had never been invited to join the group--according to the Bangladeshi policy makers. Nonetheless, Bangladesh is threatened by China. Let us think why. China knows very well that India has historically a good relationship with Bangladesh. India and Bangladesh have close socio-cultural, linguistic and economic linkages that are the outcomes common historical legacy and geographical proximity. Moreover, Bangladesh was liberated from Pakistan with support from India. When the people of Bangladesh(the then East Pakistan) were fighting against the Pakistanis, India supported her.

India supports Bangladesh not only with military means, but also at the people to people level. India, in 1971, was not economically strong, but she did not hesitate to accommodate more than 10 million refugees in West Bengal, Assam and Tripura. Despite these facts, India Bangladesh relations have experienced many ups and downs over the last 50 years; since the liberation of Bangladesh. The assassination of Bangabandhu Sheikh Mujibur Rahman, the father of the nation of Bangladesh, in 1975, was not only a severe blow to Dhaka but also to New Delhi. The military rule and the rule of anti-Indian people had a dampening effect on India-Bangladesh relations. To counter Indian rulers, the military rulers and the anti-Indian leaders were looking for China's support.

China, on the other hand, after the killing of Sheikh Mujib, not only recognized Bangladesh, it has also started deepening relations with Bangladesh.

Later when Sheikh Hasina, the daughter of Sheikh Mujib, came to power, the relations between India and Bangladesh have reached a new height again. In recent years, some long-run disputes between the two have erased with the best efforts taken by Prime Minister Narendra Modi and Sheikh Hasina. The Land Boundary Agreement is a classic example and was a major milestone in bilateral cooperation.

Both Dhaka and New Delhi know that the two are

inseparably intertwined. For the India's Northeast, Bangladesh is the India's most important neighbor and Delhi cannot ignore her. For Bangladesh, political and economic stability heavily depend on India's willingness. That is why China wants to see a cold relation between Bangladesh and India because it considers India the biggest competitor in South Asian region.

Under President Xi Jinping, China has become more nationalistic and aggressive. For economic aggression, China has rapidly modernized its defense forces and increasing its military presence in and around South Asian region. On the other hand, China is approaching the doorsteps of the developing nations and offering handful of money for their infrastructures. For that, China has embraced a new South East Asia strategy, which can be seen through the twin-track of widespread infrastructure investment across the Bay of Bengal via the Belt and Road Initiative(BRI), combined with a growing military presence. In that case, Bangladesh is being considered by China as an extra-ordinary priority. Due to that Bangladesh, a member of BRI since 2016, has received huge amounts of funding from China for infrastructure projects. The country is being lured by Chinese debt-trap, what intentionally extends excessive credit to a debtor country.

The two countries signed 27 agreements for investments and loans worth $24 billion during President Xi's Dhaka visit in 2016. Together with the $13.6 billion invested in joints ventures, Chinese investment in Bangladesh worth $38 billion. Moreover, China is playing important roles in Bangladesh's infrastructure development plans. It is building an industrial park in Chittagong port, the largest and busiest port of the country. China has also built eight friendship bridges in Bangladesh. it is also constructing railway lines, linking Bay of

Bengal port to China's Yunnan province. It has also invested $ 3.7 billion to build road and rail bridge across the Padma Bridge, which is highly sensitive for Prime Minister Sheikh Hasina's politics and hugely important to the people of southern part of the country. China is also heavily investing in energy sector. It is investing $1 billion project to digital connectivity.

Noticeably, China is trying its best to be popular inside the government of Bangladesh and to the people of the country. When the World Bank cancelled $1.2 billion credit for the Padma Bridge project, China has shown willingness to finance in the project.

Building this bridge was a political prestige for Prime Minister Sheikh Hasina and a hope to the people of the country for economic betterment. Western funders had refused to fund several projects where China came forward to assist. While Bangladesh has increasingly been involved in international business, China is regarded as the largest import partner because it contributes more than 22 percent of Bangladesh's import share. China has allowed 97 per cent of Bangladesh's export to China under its duty free, quota free programme (though it is an eyewash initiative. In Fiscal Year 2019-2020 Bangladesh exports were worth $ 831 million to China, while China exports were $13,638 million to Bangladesh).

Bangladesh is hungry for infrastructural and economical development and want Chinese businesses to invest more. Prime Minister Sheikh Hasina is convinced that the development will help her to retain power in 2024. But Bangladesh is perhaps unaware that all the Chinese activities are part of China's intention to achieve its own goal to dominate civilian maritime and transportation in South East Asia.

It seems that Chinese influence is rapidly increasing in

Bangladesh. There are some fault lines in Bangladesh and India ties, which China could try to exploit. For Bangladesh one of the discontents is Teesta River water. Being the downstream country, Bangladesh wants India to share more water from Teesta river. This is a pending agreement.

China has stepped in and offered $1 billion to Bangladesh for an irrigation project on the river Teesta. Undoubtedly Prime Minister Sheikh Hasina is the India's most trusted ally in South Asia.

Dhaka needs to be careful about China. China's closest ally in the region Pakistan has not denounced the atrocities it committed in East Pakistan during the war in 1971. Moreover, Pakistan's infamous Inter Services Intelligent (ISI) is highly active in Bangladesh. China cannot be a friend of both at a time. American President John Adams once said,' There are two ways to conquer and enslave a country, one is by the sword and the other is by debt. ' It should be remembered by the developing countries, including Bangladesh that China has not only boosted its leverage over the financially vulnerable countries but also ensnaring them in debt-trap.

A new international study (conducted by the researchers at AidData at William and Mary, the Center for Global Development, the Kiel Institute, the World Economy and the Peterson Institute for International Economics) has shed light on China's muscular and exploitative lending practices by examining 100 of its loan contracts with 24 countries, many of which participate in its Belt and Road Initiative(BRI). The study found that these agreements incorporate provisions that go beyond international lending contracts standard, that arming China with considerable leverage. According to the study, the contracts obligate the borrower to exclude the Chinese debt from any multilateral restructuring process such as the Paris club of official bilateral creditors, or from any comparable debt treatment. This is aimed at ensuring that the borrowing country remains dependent on Beijing.

Study says, many of China's loan agreements incorporate collateral arrangements, such as lender-controlled revenue accounts. Its collateralization practices seek to secure debt repayments by revenues flowing from, for example, commodity exports. Through various contract clauses, a commercially aggressive China, according to the study, limits the borrowing state's crisis management options while leveraging its own role.

There are some examples. Water-rich Laos handed China majority control of its national electric grid after its state-owned electricity company's debt spiraled to 26% of national GDP. The transfer also holds implications for national water resources as hydropower makes up more than four-fifths of Laos's total electricity generation.

A more famous example is the Sri Lankan transfer of the Hambantota Port, along with more than 6,000 hectares of land around it, to Beijing on a 99-year lease. The transfer of the Indian Ocean Region's most strategically located port in late 2017 was seen in Sri Lanka as the equivalent of a heavily indebted farmer giving away his daughter to the cruel money lender. According to Brahma Chellaney, the author of "Water: Asia's New Battleground", 'BRI, Chinese President Xi Jinping's signature initiative, has been plagued by allegations of corruption and malpractice, and many of its completed projects have proved not financially viable. After all, BRI is central to its debt-trap diplomacy. China often begins as an economic partner of a small, financially weak country and then gradually enlarges its footprint in that state to become its economic master.'

Bangladesh needs to be more careful. Bangladesh is the second-biggest receiver of Chinese investment. The infrastructural projects in Bangladesh are being carried out through dent financing. China-India relations are deteriorating, especially during the reign of President Xi Jinping. So, China hawks Bangladesh and wants to kill two birds with one stone: Making India-Bangladesh relation weaker and push Bangladesh towards debt.

(Mohshin Habib is a senior Bangladeshi author and journalist).

Chapter 4

Sino-European Ties under Xi Jinping: Model Relationship Turning Sour

– Alicja Bachulska

Throughout last decades, political and economic relations between the People's Republic of China (PRC) and the European Union (EU) have been steadily developing despite many stumbling blocks and alarm bells ringing in different European capitals every now and then. Most recently, however, dark clouds have been gathering over Sino-European ties as China's foreign policy under Xi Jinping began to reflect Beijing's newly found economic might and global ambitions. Coupled with China's increased willingness to shape international norms and standards, unconditional cooperation with Beijing now poses new threats to the EU's sovereignty, integrity and market power. European states and their civil societies have been slowly realising this fact, albeit to varying degrees and with different results. In this essay, I argue that what seems to be sure by mid-2021 is that the status quo of Sino-European relations has begun to slowly change. China's own policies at home and abroad; European politicians, researchers and journalists' efforts to shed new light on the topic as well as Europe's own evolving relations with its international partners such as the US have all influenced the process. The following chapter attempts to picture the evolution and the current shape of Sino-European relations through: 1) a brief overview of the history of EU-China cooperation; 2) a presentation of Chinese economic and political presence in the EU and its strategic implications for Europe's international standing; 3) a summary of the growing backlash against China's inroads into the EU.

HISTORY OF EU-CHINA COOPERATION AT A GLANCE

The history of relations between the PRC and the EU dates back to 1975, when official diplomatic relations between the then European Economic Community and China were established.[1] Ten years later, an agreement on trade and economic cooperation was signed and in 1988 the Delegation of the European Commission was opened in Beijing. The brutal crackdown on the Tiananmen Square protests in June 1989, however, resulted in a temporary freeze in relations and an imposition of sanctions on China by the EU, including an arms embargo, which is still valid today. Yet, it has not been legally binding, thus leaving some room for politically and economically-motivated interpretations of sanctions by various EU member states, which have resulted in some exports of dual-use items or defence equipment from Europe to China.[2] As years went by and the PRC began to emerge as a new global economic powerhouse, Sino-European ties also normalised. 1990s and 2000s witnessed a plethora of new initiatives, such

[1]"EU-China Relations: Chronology", *European External Action Service*, https://eeas.europa.eu/archives/docs/china/docs/chronology_2011_en.pdf.

[2]Jerker Hellström, "The EU Arms Embargo on China: a Swedish Perspective", *Swedish Defence Research Agency*, January 2010, https://www.foi.se/rest-api/report/FOI-R--2946--SE.

as a new bilateral political dialogue (1992), a specific dialogue on human rights (1996) or annual EU-China summits (from 1998 on).[3] In 1995, the European Commission published its first communication "A long-term policy for China-Europe relations", while eight years later (2003) the two entities announced their Comprehensive Strategic Partnership. According to their joint statement, Beijing and Brussels defined their relationship as "maturing" and enlarged their scope of cooperation to include more strategically important areas, such as non-proliferation and arms control, science and technology, industrial policies or satellite navigation cooperation, just to name a few.[4] Meanwhile, the EU supported China's accession to the World Trade Organisation (WTO) – a decisive step that had enabled Beijing's economic success story and its subsequent rise as a global power.[5] In 2004, the EU became China's biggest trading partner.[6] The inverse became true much later, in 2020, when China surpassed the US as the EU's top trade partner. Ten years after Brussels and Beijing heralded the beginning of the Comprehensive Strategic Partnership, the EU-China 2020 Strategic Agenda for Cooperation was published – another document marking the

[3]"EU-China Relations: Chronology", *European External Action Service*, https://eeas.europa.eu/archives/docs/china/docs/chronology_2011_en.pdf.

[4]Hong Zhou, "An Overview of the China-EU Strategic Partnership (2003–2013)" In: Zhou H. (eds.) *China-EU Relations. Research Series on the Chinese Dream and China's Development Path* (Singapore: Springer, 2017), p. 5.

[5]Petros C. Mavroidis and Andre Sapir, "China and the World Trade Organization: Towards a Better Fit", *Bruegel Working Paper*, Issue 06, June 11, 2019, https://www.bruegel.org/wp-content/uploads/2019/06/WP-2019-06-110619_.pdf.

[6]"China edges past US as Europe's top trade partner", *The Economic Times*, December 2, 2020, https://economictimes.indiatimes.com/news/international/business/china-edges-past-us-as-europes-top-trade-partner/articleshow/79534983.cms?from=mdr.

evolution and deepening of Sino-European economic and political interdependencies.[7] Yet again, the scope of cooperation expanded, with even more ambitious areas at the forefront, such as sustainable development and promotion of multilateralism, international peace and prosperity.

For China, its relationship with the EU was for many years considered as a "model of win-win cooperation among countries with different political systems, development processes, and civilizations".[8] Simultaneously, Beijing pushed forward regional initiatives, such as the 17+1 format (previously known as 16+1), which gathers 17 Central and Eastern European (CEE) states – both EU member states and those aspiring to join it (Western Balkan states).[9] The initiative quickly became a subject of a polarising intra-European debate on whether this kind of cooperation is conducive to the EU's integration or the opposite. In the process, many CEE states have been dubbed "Trojan horses" of EU's unity, although their level of cooperation with China has actually remained very limited compared to Western European states' level of engagement with Beijing.[10]

[7] "EU-China 2020 Strategic Agenda for Cooperation", *Delegation of the European Union to China*, November 23, 2013, https://eeas.europa.eu/sites/default/files/20131123.pdf.

[8] Dong Yifan, "Stronger China-Europe ties needed amid global uncertainty", *Global Times*, July 16, 2019, https://www.globaltimes.cn/content/1158079.shtml.

[9] Ivana Karásková, Alicja Bachulska, Agnes Szunomár, Stefan Vladisavljev (eds.), "Empty shell no more: China's growing footprint in Central and Eastern Europe", *China Observers in Central and Eastern Europe*, April 2020, https://chinaobservers.eu/wp-content/uploads/2020/04/CHOICE_Empty-shell-no-more.pdf.

[10] Alicja Bachulska, "Central and Eastern Europe is no Chinese Trojan horse", *East Asia Forum*, December 5, 2020, https://www.eastasiaforum.org/2020/12/05/central-and-eastern-europe-is-no-chinese-trojan-horse/.

All forms of cooperation and initiatives listed above have one commonality: they were rooted in a belief that engaging with China would undoubtedly bring only positive results for all partners involved. The now seemingly naïve attitude towards cooperation with Beijing from that era was a product of its times. It was rooted in a mindset which assumed that China would eventually liberalise politically once it integrates with global markets, opens up its economy and strengthens its emerging middle class. The end product of this type of thinking – the "engagement policy" – was promoted with special vigour by subsequent US administrations, especially under Bill Clinton's terms in office.[11] On both sides of the Atlantic, it took many years for representatives of liberal democracies to realise that autocracy and controlled economic opening-up might go hand in hand and actually work to the detriment of the former.

At the declarative level, from mid-1990s China devoted itself to the development of a multi-polar world and so-called win-win cooperation. For Beijing, multipolarity has become a catchphrase encapsulating its discontent towards the US-led international order and promotion of a new one, where other big players, such as China or Russia, could play a bigger role in norm-making.[12] By selectively adopting certain Western-made rules and standards on trade and investment while taking the grip over areas of economic and social life crucial to the country's stability and competitiveness, the Chinese Communist Party (CCP) has managed to strengthen its own

[11]Minxin Pei, "Is China Democratizing?", *Foreign Affairs*, Vol. 77, No. 1 (Jan. - Feb., 1998), pp. 68-82.

[12]Susan Turner, "Russia, China and a Multipolar World Order: the Danger in the Undefined", *Asian Perspective*, Vol. 33, No. 1 (2009), pp. 159-184.

political system despite relative opening-up. Moreover, the need to maintain one-party rule requires the Chinese leadership to prioritise its political and security goals over other interests. However, those are closely intertwined with China's economic development, which is one of the CCP's main sources of legitimacy. Thus, the CCP needs to constantly balance its internally and externally-conditioned existential needs, which are multidimensional and go beyond the dichotomy between politics and economics. As a result, Beijing's policies, even when trade and investment-centred, always have strategic considerations at heart. CCP-led development mechanisms, such as the Belt and Road Initiative (BRI), are also underpinned by a political culture very different than the one dominant in the EU, which stresses transparency and open dialogue, thus widening the gap in perceptions between respective European capitals and Beijing. This very gap became especially visible under Xi Jinping, when China has turned away from Deng Xiaoping's doctrine of "hiding one's capabilities and biding one's time" (*taoguangyanghui*) to adapt a new, more assertive approach towards its foreign policy, also known as "striving for achievement" (*fenfa youwei*).[13] After over eight years of Xi's rule and with limited perspectives for him transferring the power in the nearest future, Beijing's striving for power and global influence is bound to continue and have an impact on the EU.

All these elements are crucial when it comes to assessing the current state of Sino-European relations. Europe's openness to Chinese capital, coupled with the PRC's lack of the level

[13]Camilla T. N. Sørensen, "The Significance of Xi Jinping's 'Chinese Dream' for Chinese Foreign Policy: From 'Tao Guang Yang Hui' to 'Fen Fa You Wei'", *JCIR*, Vol. 3, No. 1 (2015), pp. 53-73.

playing field on its domestic market and Beijing's ability to influence European debates on China within the EU have created an asymmetric relationship between the two actors. Its implications have also revealed the continent's vulnerabilities when it comes to the future of the EU's competitiveness and attractiveness on the international arena.

CHINA'S POLITICAL AND ECONOMIC PRESENCE IN THE EU AND ITS STRATEGIC IMPLICATIONS

As described in the previous section, China and the EU have greatly intensified their cooperation throughout the 1990s and 2000s. This engagement was twofold: it occurred both in the realm of politics and economics. Political support in both Beijing and respective European capitals has created an enabling environment for growth in investments and trade. As the PRC for many years did not deploy its capital abroad, Chinese foreign direct investment (FDI) began to be watched with great interest as an indicator of Beijing's political intent and larger international strategy.[14] Between 2003 and 2009, Chinese inward investment in the EU grew from EUR 0,3 billion to EUR 4,5 billion.[15] Most of it has been located in a small number of states, mainly Germany, France and the UK.[16] After the global financial crisis of 2007-2008, Chinese investors in Europe began to focus mainly on acquisitions of brands and technologies. When it comes to the value of Chinese FDI in the EU, 2016 was a historic year with a record

[14]Jeremy Clegg, Hinrich Voss, "Chinese Overseas Direct Investment", *Europe China Research and Advice Network*, 2012, https://www.chathamhouse.org/sites/default/files/public/Research/Asia/0912ecran_cleggvoss.pdf.

[15]*Ibid.*

[16]*Ibid.*

EUR 35 billion worth of investment, compared with only EUR 1,6 billion in 2010.[17] Most of these were associated with large state-owned enterprises, although most recently their share of investments dropped significantly.[18]

Throughout the years, Chinese firms have managed to internationalise, secure access to the EU single market, acquire know-how, brands as well as technologies, and integrate with regional and global value chains.[19] These experiences have been then used by China to facilitate its domestic development towards a more advanced, higher value-added economy. The process, however, began to stir controversies in many European capitals, as China's acquisitions and the country's growing presence on the continent started to be seen not only as an opportunity but also as a potential threat. When Chinese Midea acquired the German cutting-edge robot-making company KUKA in 2016, it became "a cause célèbre" as it proved "how few tools the German government had to block an acquisition that it felt could lead to a dangerous transfer of technology".[20] Subsequent EU-wide debates on the role of the

[17]John Seaman, Mikko Huotari, Miguel Otero-Iglesias, "Chinese Investment in Europe. A Country-Level Approach", *European Think-tank Network on China*, December 2017, https://merics.org/sites/default/files/2020-04/171216_ETNC%20Report%202017_0.pdf.

[18]Agatha Kratz, Mikko Huotari, Thilo Hanemann, Rebecca Arcesati, "Chinese FDI in Europe: 2019 Update", *Mercator Institute for China Studies*, April 8, 2020, https://merics.org/sites/default/files/2020-05/MERICS Rhodium%20GroupCOFDIUpdate2020.pdf.

[19]John Seaman, Mikko Huotari, Miguel Otero-Iglesias, "Chinese Investment in Europe. A Country-Level Approach", *European Think-tank Network on China*, December 2017, https://merics.org/sites/default/files/2020-04/171216_ETNC%20Report%202017_0.pdf.

[20]Axel Höpner, Sha Hua, "Kuka kicks out CEO as Chinese shareholder seeks more investment in China", *Handelsblatt*, 27 November, 2018, https://www.handelsblatt.com/english/companies/test-case-kuka-kicks-out-ceo-as-chinese-shareholder-seeks-more-investment-in-china/23695028.html?ticket=ST-1575029-S3nFAFdWJuoIffQPYZfB-ap4.

Chinese state in the country's economy began to reflect growing distrust towards Chinese companies, their motifs as well as their ties to the CCP.

The asymmetry of relations between the PRC and the EU came to the forefront of the discussion, with multiple calls to level the playing field between the two actors in order to reduce China's unfair advantage in the EU market.[21] Contentious issues emerged both in relation to investments as well as trade. In years 2000-2019, the volume of trade between China and the EU grew almost eightfold to EUR 560 billion.[22] However, this very growth has been unbalanced to the PRC's advantage, leading to large trade deficits both at the EU level and in most EU member states. This way, overdependence on imports from China has become another cornerstone of the debate on Sino-European relations. The problem became especially pressing at the beginning of the COVID-19 pandemic, when Chinese manufacturers halted most of the country's production, which disrupted global value chains and caused serious problems for the European economy.[23] Over the years, the EU's concerns kept on growing, encompassing issues such as continued lack of reciprocity; intellectual property rights violations; forced

[21]Alicia García-Herrero, Guntram B. Wolff, "China Has an Unfair Advantage in the EU Market. What Can Be Done to Level the Playing Field?", *Bruegel*, July 28, 2020, https://www.bruegel.org/2020/07/china-has-an-unfair-advantage-in-the-eu-market-what-can-be-done-to-level-the-playing-field/.

[22]Max J. Zenglein, "Mapping and recalibrating Europe's economic interdependence with China", *Mercator Institute for China Studies*, November 17, 2020, https://merics.org/en/report/mapping-and-recalibrating-europes-economic-interdependence-china.

[23]Laurens Cerulus, "Coronavirus forces Europe to confront China dependency", *Politico*, March 6, 2020, https://www.politico.eu/ article/ coronavirus-emboldens-europes-supply-chain-security-hawks/.

technology transfer; deteriorating human rights situation (mostly in Xinjiang and Tibet) and lack of respect for rules-based international order (e.g., imposition of the new national security law in Hong Kong).

All the problems mentioned above became crucial in the negotiations of the long-awaited Comprehensive Agreement on Investment (CAI) between China and the EU. Although Beijing has concluded Bilateral Investment Treaties (BITs) with 26 out of 27 EU member states, their terms and clauses have varied significantly, with some of them being already outdated.[24] Thus, in order to unify its approach throughout all of its member states, in 2012 a political agreement was reached between Brussels and Beijing and a year later the European Commission began negotiating an EU-wide investment agreement with the PRC. Throughout eight years, over 30 rounds of negotiations seemed not to have delivered what Brussels had envisioned for the agreement. The breakthrough came on December 30, 2020, when the European Commission suddenly announced that the EU and China had concluded in principle the negotiations for CAI. The decision stirred many controversies, as it appeared premature and instrumental to Merkel's China policy, especially in the context of the ending German EU presidency at the end of 2020.[25] For many German stakeholders, such as the country's powerful automakers, maintaining the current status quo in relations with China

[24]Liming Wang and Yuan Li,"The Negotiation of EU-China Comprehensive Agreement on Investment and its Potential Impact in the Post-Pandemic Era", *Journal of Chinese Economic and Business Studies*, Vol. 18, No. 4 (2020), pp. 365-372.

[25]Theresa Fallon, "The Strategic Implications of the China-EU Investment Deal", *The Diplomat*, January 4, 2021, https://thediplomat.com/2021/01/the-strategic-implications-of-the-china-eu-investment-deal/.

seems beneficial. Since then, CAI has been countlessly criticised for being an instrument further cementing Beijing's advantage vis-à-vis Brussels. Its provisions have been accused of being too vague and many have pointed towards the timing of the agreement (i.e., right before Joe Biden took office as the new US president) and its detrimental effect for transatlantic relations' shape and China-related strategic dialogue. It has been also pointed out that CAI does not address highly sensitive political issues that are part of investment relations with China – instead, it is a rather conventional and not very sophisticated market access deal.[26]

For many less influential European countries, such as Poland, Italy or Spain, CAI's hasty conclusion seem to reflect the interests of the most powerful interest groups from the strongest EU states like Germany and France.[27] These voices have also been symptomatic when it comes to growing fears in many European capitals of the EU's China policy being jeopardised by the Franco-German tandem. As Gudrun Wacker and François Godement have pointed out, "Germany has a stronger sense of identification with the EU and better capacity to 'lead' on China-related issues than France, but it remains cautious for historical reasons".[28] Nevertheless, these

[26]Christina Gigler, "EU-China Comprehensive Agreement on Investment (CAI)", *Rödl & Partner*, February 18, 2021, https://www.roedl.com/insights/cai-china-eu-investment-comprehensive-agreement-facilitated-market-access.

[27]Jakob Hanke Vela, Giorgio Leali and Barabara Moens, "Germany's drive for EU-China deal draws criticism from other EU countries", *Politico*, January 1, 2021, https://www.politico.eu/article/germanys-drive-for-eu-china-deal-draws-criticism-from-other-eu-countries/.

[28]François Godement and Gudrun Wacker, "France and Germany Together. Promoting a European China Policy", *Institut Montaigne*, November 2020, https://www.institutmontaigne.org/en/publications/promoting-european-china-policy-france-and-germany-together.

two countries have the biggest potential and bargaining power vis-à-vis China. Yet, their own economic interests seem to be still paramount in their policymaking, rather than their own role in promoting a stronger, more comprehensive China policy that would consider a multitude of voices as well as strategic considerations regarding the EU's future and global standing. Berlin has been the loudest advocate of policy compartmentalisation regarding China: it has defended the view that economic and political relations can be developed independently from each other and without detriment to the EU's overall bargaining position. Yet, many in Europe have diverging views on the matter.

GROWING BACKLASH AGAINST CHINA'S INROADS INTO THE EU

The political realities of Sino-European ties in the last decade has forced the EU to turn towards a more realistic assessment of costs and benefits of cooperation with the PRC. In 2017, when the European Council on Foreign Relations (ECFR) conducted its second audit of China's power in relations with the EU, it has concluded that "Europe is now turning towards realist engagement with China, getting over the temptation of cash from China. China is strengthening its command economy, turning to full state-led industry and technology policies, including its military applications. In Europe, this means acquisition of critical technologies, scientific cooperation agreements mirroring China 2025 goals, and other massive plans to lead the fourth industrial revolution".[29] These

[29] Francois Godement and Abigaël Vasselier, "China at the Gates. A New Power Audit of EU-China Relations", *European Council on Foreign Relations*, December 2017, https://ecfr.eu/wp-content/uploads/China_Power_Audit.pdf.

assertions have been reflected in the European Commission's joint communication to the European Parliament, the European Council and the Council from March 2019, also known as the EU-China Strategic Outlook.[30] In the document, the Commission has stated that "there is a growing appreciation in Europe that the balance of challenges and opportunities presented by China has shifted".[31] Moreover, for the first time in the history of Sino-European ties, the PRC was named not only a cooperation partner, but also an "economic competitor in the pursuit of technological leadership" and a "systemic rival promoting alternative models of governance".[32] To a significant degree, many in the EU have become weary of China's lack of significant progress in implementing its long-promised market reforms and the CCP's strengthening of control over the private sector.[33] Last but not least, with growing reports of human rights abuses against the Uyghur minority in the region of Xinjiang and Beijing's ongoing crackdown on civil liberties throughout the country, long-sidelined normative issue have also returned to the core of the debate.

All these elements have increased uncertainty regarding Beijing's ability to deliver and accommodate the EU's interests, also in the context of the previously-mentioned Comprehensive

[30]"EU-China – A strategic outlook", *European Commission*, March 12, 2019, https://ec.europa.eu/info/sites/default/files/communication-eu-china-a-strategic-outlook.pdf.

[31]*Ibid.*

[32]*Ibid.*

[33]Damian Wnukowski (PISM), Marek Wąsiński (PIE) (eds.), "EU-China Comprehensive Agreement on Investment: Political and Economic Implications for the European Union", *Polish Institute of International Affairs*, 2021, https://pism.pl/publikacje/EUCHINA_COMPREHENSIVE__AGREEMENT_ON_INVESTMENT__POLITICAL_AND_ECONOMIC_IMPLICATIONS__FOR_THE_EUROPEAN_UNION.

Agreement on Investment. In May 2021, the European Parliament voted to suspend CAI's ratification, with the motion passed by 599 votes, with 30 votes against and 58 abstentions.[34] The move was not only a reflection of the EU-wide dissatisfaction with the current shape of the agreement, but also a response to China's retaliatory sanctions on the EU officials, academics and researchers. These were related to the EU's earlier sanctions from March 2021, targeting Chinese officials engaged in human rights abuses in Xinjiang, where according to reports over one million ethnic Uyghurs have been detained and subject to forced labour.[35] From the European perspective, Beijing's retaliation was disproportionate as it targeted not only on politicians, but also civil society members, thus explicitly showcasing China's ambitions to influence the shape of democratic debates and knowledge-making processes within the EU.

Changes in China policies in many CEE states are a good example of the evolution of European attitudes towards the government in Beijing. While some of them have supported Chinese interests by trying to block or water down EU criticism of China's actions (to score political points in Beijing in hope of them turning into inflow of Chinese investment), many of them have actually moved to the forefront of a more critical debate about the desired outcomes of Sino-European cooperation.[36]

[34]Stuart Lau, "European Parliament votes to 'freeze' investment deal until China lifts sanctions", *Politico*, May 20, 2021, https://www.politico.eu/article/european-parliament-freezes-china-investment-deal-vote/amp/.

[35]Lindsay Maizland, "China's Repression of Uyghurs in Xinjiang", *Council on Foreign Relations*, March 1, 2021, https://www.cfr.org/backgrounder/chinas-repression-uyghurs-xinjiang.

[36]Filip Šebok, "The Slow Demise of 'Business as Usual' in China-EU Relations", *China Observers in Central and Eastern Europe*, May 5, 2021, https://chinaobservers.eu/the-slow-demise-of-business-as-usual-in-china-eu-relations/.

With the exception of Hungary, which still bets on China as its strategic partner within the "Opening to the East" policy, countries such as Czechia, Slovakia or Lithuania have been sending signals of disenchantment with the lack of results of economic cooperation with China and the political costs of their engagement with an authoritarian regime. For example, Czechia has significantly extended its ties with Taiwan,[37] an island considered by Beijing as a renegade province, while Lithuania left the 17+1 format after months of considerations whether the initiative had brought any tangible benefits for the country. Moreover, the country's parliament deemed China's treatment of Uyghurs as amounting to "genocide" and "crime against humanity".[38] In late May 2021, Lithuanian foreign minister stated that "there is no such thing as 17+1 anymore, as for practical purposes Lithuania is out", adding that "it is high time for the EU to move from a dividing 16+1 format to a more uniting and therefore much more efficient 27+1".[39] The latter format has been suggested multiple times, for example by Berlin during its presidency at the Council of the European Union in the second half of 2020. However, the COVID-19 pandemic did not enable such a format to materialize yet. Meanwhile, Lithuania's decision to limit its presence within the 17+1

[37]Dominika Remžová, "The Czech Model: A New Era for Taiwan's Diplomacy in Europe?", November 13, 2020, *China Observers in Central and Eastern Europe*, https://chinaobservers.eu/the-czech-model-a-new-era-for-taiwans-diplomacy-in-europe/.

[38]"Lithuanian parliament passes resolution condemning 'Uighur genocide' in China", *Lithuanian Radio and Television*, May 20, 2021, https://www.lrt.lt/en/news-in-english/19/1413940/lithuanian-parliament-passes-resolution-condemning-uyghur-genocide-in-china.

[39]Stuart Lau, "Lithuania pulls out of China's '17+1' bloc in Eastern Europe", *Politico*, May 21, 2021, https://www.politico.eu/article/lithuania-pulls-out-china-17-1-bloc-eastern-central-europe-foreign-minister-gabrielius-landsbergis/.

platform has met fierce criticism from the Chinese side, with some state-affiliated media pushing patronizing narratives on the country's performance fitting well "with the Chinese idiom: 'contemptible scoundrel'".[40] This kind of language has been recently pervasive not only in Chinese media, but also in its diplomatic rhetoric. The so-called "wolf warrior diplomacy" has been yet another element that negatively impacted China's image in Europe, with multiple Chinese diplomats engaging in public debates while using especially strong and oftentimes even intimidating language.

Another dimension of changing attitudes towards China throughout the EU are public sentiments towards the government in Beijing. According to the latest survey conducted in September and October 2020 in 13 European countries, China is seen increasingly negatively in most of them, with Sweden, Germany, France, the Czech Republic among those most sceptical.[41] When it comes to specific areas of cooperation, only trade is seen positively in most of the surveyed countries, while China's impact on democracy in other countries as well as on the global environment appear as the most negatively perceived issues.[42] Bearing these results in mind, European politicians will probably focus increasingly on how the public responds to respective governments' attempts to shape their China policies. As political polarisation grows across Europe, it might be expected that it will also translate into more radical positions on China throughout European societies.

[40]"Lithuania risks trouble with geopolitical move: Global Times editorial", *Global Times*, May 23, 2021, https://www.globaltimes.cn/page/202105/1224253.shtml.

[41]Richard Q. Turcsányi, Matej Šimalčík, Kristína Kironská, Renáta Sedláková et al. "European public opinion on China in the age of COVID-19", *CEIAS / Sinophone Borderlands*, 2020, https://ceias.eu/wp-content/uploads/2020/11/COMP-poll-report_3.pdf.

CONCLUSIONS

As Janka Oertel from ECFR has noted, "since the onset of the COVID-19 crisis, there has been a new convergence of EU member states' assessment of the challenges China poses to Europe. The Sino-European economic relationship lacks reciprocity, and there are mounting concerns within the EU about China's assertive approach abroad, as well as its breaches of international legal commitments and massive violations of human rights in Hong Kong and Xinjiang."[43] It seems that the EU has been set on creating a new toolbox of defensive measures aimed at securing the EU single market in the face of changing global balance of power. However, the process will be very difficult, as the Lisbon Treaty requires unanimity within the European Council or the Council when it comes to foreign policy.[44] Moreover, deciding upon a common stance and shared interests becomes even more difficult given that only a few European states have their dedicated China policy. In this context, the future of a coordinated, EU-wide approach towards China remains problematic. Yet, the topic is here to stay as China's gradual rise to the position of a global superpower seems to continue. Intra-European debates and resulting policies, as well as the closeness of ties with other like-minded nations will

[42]Ibid.

[43]Janka Oertel, "The new China consensus: How Europe is growing wary of Beijing", *European Council on Foreign Relations*, September 7, 2020, https://ecfr.eu/publication/the_new_china_consensus_how_europe_is_growing_wary_of_beijing/.

[44]Grzegorz Stec, "Power from Within: The Benchmark for EU Unity on China", *China Observers in Central and Eastern Europe*, November 24, 2020, https://chinaobservers.eu/power-from-within-the-benchmark-of-the-eus-unity-on-china/.

determine the EU's competitiveness and global standing for the decades to come. The process should be watched carefully as it can offer important insights into how small and medium-sized countries can cooperate in order to retain their autonomy vis-à-vis rising authoritarian powers.

(Alicja Bachulska is China analyst with Asia Research Centre (War Studies University), Warsaw. She tweets @a_bachulska)

Chapter 5

China's Schizophrenic Diplomacy in Europe

– Kelly Alkhouli

Over the past two decades, the world order has steadily shifted away from American and European influence. Inconsistent strategies and failed military interventions, most notably in Afghanistan and Iraq, have hindered American hegemony. Meanwhile, European nations have retreated from international politics and are struggling to cope with the consequences of the COVID-19 pandemic. As we enter an increasingly multi-polar world order, China – under Xi Jinping's rule - is determined to take advantage of the divide and decline of the West in order to expand its sphere of influence and solidify its place on the international stage.

The most remarkable shift in China's foreign policy has been the modern revival of the ancient Silk Road, announced in 2013 by President Xi Jinping in Nur-Sultan, Kazakhstan. The Belt and Road

Initiative is comprised of two aspects: the Silk Road Economic Belt and the 21st Century Maritime Silk Road. Both aspects aim to connect China to the world through numerous infrastructure projects in Central Asia, South Asia, the Middle

East, Africa and Europe in order to support Chinese export flows. The BRI is a $1 trillion vision that allows China to exert influence through its economic leverage. Furthermore, the BRI has key domestic benefits by redirecting excess domestic capacity and capital, most notably in steel and cement, towards these oversees infrastructure projects. It also allows Chinese firms to gain a more prominent presence across the world whilst requiring Chinese workers to be used for the construction of most of these projects. Beijing has also focused on increasing cooperation within existing international institutions and has worked on creating new institutions that bypass the United States, such as the Asian Infrastructure Investment Bank (AIIB), the New Development Bank (NDB) and the Shanghai Cooperation Organisation (SCO). China's use of soft power is meant to appease international fears that its political and economic rise will disturb the world order and result in violent consequences.

Beijing has sought to strengthen economic ties and maintain a position of neutrality on various foreign policy issues in order to assuage western and neighbouring countries. Before announcing the BRI, China launched the 16+1 initiative in 2012 with an aim of promoting economic relations between China and 16 countries of Central and Eastern Europe (CEE). This later became the 17+1, with the addition of Greece in 2019. The initiative was initially welcomed with open arms and enthusiasm, with the announcement of numerous projects and investments in infrastructure and the energy sector in the region. While many speculated that this new initiative would represent a gateway for China into Europe, and potentially cause greater geopolitical divisions within the continent, we can see that nearly nine years after its launch the initiative has only resulted in a series of unfulfilled promises, antagonising most members.

One of the key flagship projects of the 16+1 cooperation is the Budapest-Belgrade railway, announced in 2013, and the first BRI project in Europe. It serves as a key component of the BRI as it is part of the route linking the Port of Piraeus in Greece to Budapest and connecting the Balkans to the European Union, therefore facilitating access to the common market. 85% of the construction costs is to be financed by the Export-Import Bank of China through a 20-year loan of $1.8 billion to Hungary and $1.3 billion to Serbia. The project has yet to be implemented but has already drawn sharp criticisms within Hungary over fears of ending up in a debt-trap. Prime Minister Viktor Orban's close ties with China has united and strengthened Hungary's opposition parties. In an open letter addressed to Xi Jinping, the six leading opposition candidates have pledged to immediately halt the railway link if elected in 2022.

Within Europe, China's debt-trap diplomacy is most prominent in Montenegro, serving as a cautionary tale for neighbouring countries. With a GDP of roughly $5.5 billion, Montenegro must pay the first instalment of the $1 billion loan from the Chinese state bank, even though less than a quarter of the highway has been built. The project has been marred with corruption allegations and is leading to a rise in anti-china sentiment. Despite their debt to China, Montenegro is more interested in strengthening ties with the West, as seen through their decision to join NATO in 2017 and their continued commitment to joining the European Union.

In fact, Beijing is facing difficulties in developing most of their projects in the region. Despite signing agreements on a dozen projects in Romania's energy sector in 2013, which would amount to an investment of $10 billion, none of their projects have materialised. After 6 years of negotiations, the Romanian government has decided to abandon their agreement with China General Nuclear Power (CGN) regarding the construction of two nuclear reactors at the Cernavoda Nuclear Power Plant. Furthermore, due to numerous delays, unfulfilled promises and political pressure, Bucharest took the decision to ban Chinese companies from major infrastructure projects. A similar situation arose in Czech Republic, with CGN being excluded from taking part in a tender to build the Dukovany Nuclear Power Plant. Chinese involvement is seen as more of an obstacle than an asset.

China's cooperation with Central and Eastern European countries showed great promise at the start, yet the failures of most of their projects has led to members feeling disillusioned by the initiative and in some instances, a rise in anti-China sentiment. Lithuania has even decided to withdraw from the initiative in May 2021 and has urged other countries to do the same. Moreover, many Central and Eastern European countries are staunch allies of the United States, due to economic and geopolitical reasons, therefore are unwilling to jeopardise their ties with Washington over China. A number of these countries have even joined the United States in adopting a hardline position against Huawei's access to their 5G networks.

One of the countries in Europe where China has found some success in its development of the BRI has been Greece, for the time being. Struggling with the aftermath of the financial crisis of 2008, which led to the Greek debt crisis, Athens welcomed Chinese investments. In 2016, China's shipping company COSCO purchased a majority stake in the Piraeus Port and announced plans of investing 600 million euros. The objective is to transform the Piraeus Port into the largest transit hub between Europe and Asia. By deepening economic ties, Greece has adopted a more favourable stance regarding China within the European Union. In 2017, Greece blocked an EU statement criticising human rights records in China and in July 2021, Prime Minister Mitsotakis accepted Beijing's invitation to attend the 2022 Winter Olympics held in China, even though the European Parliament has called for a diplomatic boycott.

It is becoming increasingly challenging for the European Union to adopt a common stance in regards to China. German Chancellor Angela Merkel has been cautious to not antagonise Beijing and risk damaging economic ties. Under the German EU presidency of 2020, China and the EU passed the Comprehensive Agreement on Investment (CAI), an ambitious agreement that aims to provide EU investors with greater access to China's consumer market and allow them to compete on a better level playing field in China. However, relations between the EU and China have since deteriorated. In March 2021, the European Union, United Kingdom, Canada and the United States imposed sanctions on certain Chinese officials in Xinjiang over human rights abuses against the Uighur minority. Beijing quickly retaliated by sanctioning four EU entities and 10 individuals, including members of the European Parliament, for "maliciously spreading lies and false information." This led to members of the European Parliament voting to freeze the EU-China CAI until sanctions are lifted. Given that Germany pushed through the investment agreement with China in the final days of its presidency – despite concerns by other member states - it now finds itself in a delicate position. During her last visit to Washington in July, Merkel reiterated her unwillingness to enter in a Cold War with Beijing, especially since China is Germany's largest trading partner. The German automotive industry is becoming increasingly dependent on the Chinese market, with Volkswagen selling 40% of its vehicles in China. On the other hand, many German companies are becoming increasingly wary of Beijing's growing influence. The Federation of German Industries (BDI), an influential confederation of German industries, has repeatedly criticised China's aggressive position and has called for a strengthening of the EU's commitments to compete with China.

With Merkel soon leaving office, it remains unclear whether Germany will maintain a softer stance on China. Chinese influence within a European country is heavily dependent on internal politics and changes in power. Under Giuseppe Conte, Italy had improved relations with China and was the first G7 country to sign an MOU supporting the Belt and Road Initiative in 2019. However, many projects and collaborations did not materialise and Italian companies found that the agreement had not facilitated access to the Chinese market. After Mario Draghi took office in February 2021, Italy adopted a tougher stance on China and proclaimed wanting to "reset China ties on more equal footing". Draghi's government has imposed restrictions on Huawei's development of 5G networks, vetoed the Shenzhen Investment Holding Company from buying a controlling stake in an Italian semiconductor company and has taken a more resolute stance denouncing human rights abuses in China.

Meanwhile, France has attempted to strike a more balanced tone against China. President Emmanuel Macron has called against European naivety in regards to China, yet he has been hesitant to join US President Joe Biden in developing a program to rival the Chinese Communist Party's (CCP) BRI. France, like many other countries, is struggling to cope with the economic ramifications of months of lockdown due to the pandemic. While there are clear economic benefits to increasing ties with China, Beijing's belligerent attitude has encumbered relations with many EU members. The CCP's initial use of soft power had greater success in gaining influence within Europe. Yet now, faced with deteriorating relations with the United States and mounting international criticisms over human rights abuses in Xinjiang and Hong Kong, Beijing has shifted to intimidation and aggression. Over the past years, China has encouraged "wolf-warrior diplomats" to praise the Chinese government and attack individuals, organisations and governments who appear hostile or critical towards China. The Chinese Ambassador in France, Lu Shaye, had to be summoned on three separate occasions due to insulting comments and threats. The latest incident involved the Ambassador calling a French researcher Antoine Bondaz, a "small-time thug" and "mad hyena" on Twitter. The first incident occurred a year earlier in April 2020, when the Chinese embassy published an article defending China's response to the pandemic and made baseless accusations suggesting that care-workers in Western nursing homes had abandoned their jobs, leaving residents to die. The article also falsely claimed that Taiwanese authorities and French parliamentarians co-signed a declaration attacking the directorgeneral of the WHO, Dr Tedros Adhanom Ghebreyesus, while using a racial slur.

Moreover, in an effort to deflect from the origins and lack of transparency regarding China's handling of COVID-19, the CCP has blamed Kazakhstan, Spain, Italy and finally the United States for the spread of the pandemic. In doing so, China needlessly angered some of its allies and ended up undermining their mask and vaccine diplomacy in Spain and Italy. Beijing's attempt at balancing hard power with soft power comes off as schizophrenic diplomacy, which will prove detrimental to its interests in the long-run.

China's wolf-warrior diplomacy is an effective intimidation tactic that panders to the CCP's propaganda, yet it's a counterproductive strategy as it hampers public opinion over China and alienates potential allies. Beijing saw its relations with Norway deteriorate when it decided to sanction Norway after the Norwegian Nobel Committee awarded the 2010 Nobel Peace Prize to Liu Xiaobo – a Chinese Human Rights Activist who took part in the Tiananmen Square protests of 1989. Similarly, China's relations with Sweden soured when a Swedish literary organization,

Svenska PEN, awarded the Tucholsky Prize in 2019 to Gui Minhai, a Hong Kong bookseller with Swedish citizenship who has been abducted and detained by China. The Chinese ambassador to Sweden then threatened to ban the Swedish Minister of Culture, Amanda Lin, from entering China if she dared attend the Svenska PEN's award ceremony. Beijing has now turned against Lithuania with vague ominous threats after the latter announced the opening of a "Taiwan Representative Office" in Vilnius.

While China previously tried to work within international institutions and frameworks to gain greater influence and discreetly shape the world order to their advantage, their efforts have been severely sabotaged by their increasingly aggressive rhetoric and foreign policy. One of the catalysts for this sudden change has been reneging of their international agreement with the United Kingdom regarding Hong Kong. After a year of pro-democracy protests in Hong Kong, Beijing imposed the National Security Law in 2020, undermining the "one country, two systems" arrangement. The CCP has now consolidated control over Hong Kong, curbed freedom of speech and imprisoned political dissidents. The UK demonstrated a timid response by merely condemning China's actions. While the UK has facilitated a path to British citizenship for individuals fleeing Hong Kong under a new visa scheme, it has also advocated forging closer ties with China in the wake of Brexit. The lack of geopolitical consequences for China has emboldened them. On the 100th anniversary of the CCP on July 1st 2021, in a bellicose and nationalist speech Xi proclaimed that China will not be "oppressed" or allow "sanctimonious preaching" and threatened that anyone who dares try to do so "will have their heads bashed bloody against the Great Wall of Steel forged by over 1.4 billion Chinese people". We are witnessing a return to Mao's cult of personality with Xi Jinping, where party loyalty has become synonymous to patriotism. The CCP is enforcing mass surveillance and censorship while pursuing forced sincization programs, especially in Xinjiang and Tibet. Fearful of separatists and antigovernment protests in mainland China, the CCP has down on personal freedoms internally while using an ultranationalist rhetoric to consolidate power.

Geopolitical tensions are rising once again with the potential threat of a Chinese invasion of Taiwan. In a propaganda video, the CCP has even openly threatened to use nuclear weapons against Japan if they attempted to protect Taiwan in case of an invasion. In spite of China's utter disregard of international norms and rules, Europe as a whole has failed to develop a robust strategy against China's expansionist agenda. Fundamentally, this displays a loss of influence that many European nations have been gradually experiencing over the past decades.

Essentially, the European Union is unable to adopt a united front against China due to diverging economic interests and a decline in the European ideal. The Eurozone crisis has led to increased EU skepticism, which has been exacerbated with the migrant crisis, Brexit and the mishandling of COVID-19. The pandemic has demonstrated a lack of solidarity and leadership within the European Union, with members unilaterally shutting borders and stealing personal protective equipment (PPE) from one another. Furthermore, the initial failures of the EU vaccination campaign have fuelled EU skepticism and as a result we are witnessing a rise in populist leaders who advocate for greater nationalism. The European Union also suffers from structural challenges. This has also prevented member states from developing their independent foreign policy, leading to an overall retreat from the international stage. On the one hand, many EU members feel a disequilibrium of power within the EU, with policies catering more to the interests of France and Germany in particular. On the other hand, the EU requires unanimity amongst its 27 members in order to reach a decision, which often times leads to no decision. This has often led to EU countries turning to the US for leadership, especially in geopolitics. From a pragmatic perspective, European nations are now reluctant to blindly follow the US and sacrifice their economic interests with China. The Trump presidency has severely damaged transatlantic relations. The US have proven that their position on international politics, and their alliance with European nations, could easily change within the span of four years.

Ultimately, the EU should develop its own strategy regarding China on foreign policy and economics – independent from the US. This should include a tougher stance against China's human rights abuses and their wolf warrior diplomats, greater restrictions against Huawei and their development of 5G networks as well as stricter oversight of technology transfers and Chinese investments. The Belt and Road Initiative isn't a comprehensive strategy but a vague concept that China has been improvising for the past decade. It's one of the reasons why many BRI projects in Europe have failed. It's folly to believe that Beijing holds the upper hand, they remain heavily dependent on the EU economically.

(Kelly Alkhouli is the Director of International Relations Center of Political and Foreign Affairs, Europe).

Chapter 6

Resetting the Relationship: Changes in Britain's Foreign Policy towards China in the 21st Century

– Duncan Bartlett

Few British prime ministers have been as dismissive of the policies of their predecessors as Boris Johnson. After becoming leader of the Conservative Party in the summer of 2019, he performed a series of 360 degree U-turns on schemes set out by previous prime ministers Theresa May (2016 to 2019) and David Cameron (2010 to 2016), both of whom were also Conservatives.

Most dramatically, Mr Johnson cast aside a close relationship with the European Union – an approach which was the direct opposite to that advocated by David Cameron and was also far more confrontational than that of Theresa May. Johnson showed utter determination to press ahead with Britain's exit from the union, following a referendum on the issue in 2017.

This caused angry scenes in parliament and led to street protests. Mr Johnson also endured criticism from much of the media, with some members of his own party condemning him in the press. Even judges and bishops labelled his actions illegal or sinful. Nevertheless, Mr Johnson's belligerence earned him the reputation of a tough leader and helped him win a landslide victory in the British general election of December 2019.

Britain's shift in foreign policy towards China has been almost as profound as the change in its approach to Europe. Where once a Conservative British government insisted that China was a land of opportunity and a trusted business partner, by 2021, the tone had turned adversarial.

The review of defence, security and foreign policy issued in March 2021 – titled Global Britain in a Competitive Age – stated that China's rise is the "biggest state-based threat" to the UK's economic security and presents a "systemic challenge" to Britain.

The response to this "threat" has been varied. In the business field, a lucrative deal with the Chinese telecoms firm Huawei was terminated. On the diplomatic front, opponents of Chinese communism from Hong Kong were offered visas and work opportunities in the UK.

There was also a tilt towards Asia in the deployment of the British armed forces. A Royal Navy aircraft carrier strike group was despatched to patrol the South China Sea. The Foreign Secretary made it clear that in the event of war in Asia, the British army would join sides with the United States in fighting China. A new battery of nuclear missiles, capable of infiltrating Beijing's defences, was commissioned.

In this chapter, we will look at some of the key factors which led to this significant change in policy and consider how the Chinese government views Britain and Europe.

Let us begin with the story of a schoolgirl named Liberty Kate Osborne, who spent part of her childhood near the seat of power at Westminster. Her father, George Osborne, was

Chancellor of the Exchequer, a rather antiquated title used to describe the British finance minister. This prestigious job landed him a family home at Number 11 Downing Street, next to that of the Prime Minister, David Cameron, who lived at Number 10.

When she was twelve years old, Liberty would return home from school, climb the stairs to the ministerial flat and do her Mandarin homework every night. We know this because her father boasted of her commitment to learning Chinese when he made a fulsome speech praising China at the Shanghai Stock Exchange in 2015.

Osborne said Shanghai had become one of the great centres of the world economy. He lauded China's economic development, saying that its leaders had lifted "500 million Chinese citizens out of the grinding poverty their families have lived in since time immemorial – the biggest single contribution to making poverty history in my lifetime."

This interpretation, which overlooks the ruinous setback to economic progress caused by Chairman Mao's Cultural Revolution, fits neatly with the patriotic rhetoric which the Chinese Communist Party uses to legitimise its hold on power. Mr Osborne also called China "a great civilisation" and spoke of a win-win relationship between the two countries.

The Chinese were delighted. Glowing reports of the speech appeared on the front pages of newspapers such as Global Times and China Daily. A grand feast was prepared in Shanghai. The following morning, Mr Osbourne was flown first class to Xinjiang province in the far west of China, the first senior member of the British government to be invited to the region.

That part of the trip was pretty much ignored by the British press but its significance was clear to China. Following a spate of terrorist attacks by separatist groups from Xinjiang, Xi Jinping was determined to show his control over the province. Taking a foreign VIP there was a display of influence and power, especially a friendly figure from a mature Western democracy. The early stages of a crackdown Muslim Uigher minority were already underway but kept hidden from view. In 2015, Xi Jinping appointed Chen Quanguo as leader of the Communist Party in the province. On Chen's orders, detention camps, known as re-education centres, were introduced.

The scale of the prison system was made clear in a BBC documentary which was broadcast in 2018. The programme, Panorama, presented by John Sudworth, accused China of locking up hundreds of thousands of Muslims without trial in Xinjiang. Later, BBC news and current affairs journalists managed to get interviews with many people who claimed they had been tortured by their Chinese guards. The issue soon became the focus of a major international human rights campaign. Ministers from the British government were pressed for a response in TV interviews. They were asked to explain why Britain was showing friendships to a Chinese regime which was showing an increasingly authoritarian streak.

I noticed at first hand how deeply the reports about Xinjiang had upset politicians from all parties in the United Kingdom. There was anger and frustration at the meetings I attended about Xinjiang in the House of Commons. I also attended briefings for politicians and journalists at which Uigher representatives suggested that ethnic cleansing or even genocide was taking place. MPs from across the political spectrum said they were shocked but it was often politicians from the Conservative party who were the most ready to condemn China.

China was also rising to the top of the agenda in the United States with Donald Trump in the White House. President

Trump insisted that China's sharp trade practices were costing American livelihoods and harming the US economy. He sought revenge through tariffs and sanctions. He appointed two national security advisors, HR McMaster and later John Bolton, who warned of China's threat to international security. They emphasised the risk of war breaking out between China and America or one of its allies. The view from Washington was that China's Communist system was a mounting threat to the values of democracy and its leader, Xi Jinping, was portrayed as a tyrant. There was a strong diplomatic push, especially under Mr Trump's Secretary of State Mike Pompeo, to rally America's allies to the cause. It would be seen as a test of loyalty for Boris Johnson. The Americans wanted to know clearly which side he supported in the great power rivalry.

By the time Trump and Pompeo were on their crusade, former Prime Minister Carmeron and other friends of China had been banished to the political wilderness. George Osbourne's 2015 Shanghai speech – entitled "Let's create a golden decade for the UK-China relationship" – had become an embarrassment to the Conservative party and its tone was an anathema to the Trump administration.

In 2020, the Conservative MPs Tom Tugendhat and Neil O'Brien founded a group in parliament known as the China Research Group, which pressed the government to take a much more robust line on China. Its members agreed with Mr Trump's view that like-minded democractic countries should stand united in the face of China's rise.

Mike Pompeo raised his concerns about Xinjiang at a meeting with Prime Minister Johnson and the Foreign Secretary Dominic Raab in Downing Street in the summer of 2020. A Pentagon official described the detention centres in Xinjiang as "concentration camps". President Trump signed the Uyghur Human Rights Policy Act in 2020, although his former national security advisor John Bolton claims that privately, Mr Trump told Xi Jinping he admired his tough approach and advised him to build more camps.

After the UK left the EU at the end of January 2020, the UK government wanted to show that it could take a less Eurocentric approach to international affairs. Prime Minister Johnson said that the United Kingdom should create a fruitful network of trade, diplomatic and security relationships which could flourish outside the EU. He called the concept "Global Britain."

This led to a political process known as the Integrated Review, through which the government used its Conservative MPs and their advisors to draw up a vision for Britain's place in the world, post-Brexit.

Despite the turbulent mood caused by Donald Trump, the British government decided there would be no compromise on the alliance with the United States. The Integrated Review concluded that the UK should be the strongest and most reliable ally of America in Europe, regardless of whether a Republican or a Democrat held office in the White House.

Pressed by the right wing of the Conservative party, the government agreed to an increase in defence spending, despite the strain on the economy caused by the Covid pandemic. The government also reduced its overseas aid budget, a decision which was condemned by several previous Conservative leaders, including former prime minister Thersa May. Such divisive decisions indicated the strong influence of the China Research Group on government policy.

The Johnson government sought trade deals and security links with countries which are rivals to China, especially India and Japan. The government said it would deepen Britain's links to democratic Asian countries, which have the potential for strong economic growth and are markets for British exports. The UK pledged to "encourage liberal values in Asian countries which are on a development trajectory."

Tom Tugendhat, Chair of the Foreign Affairs Committee and founder of the China Research Group, explained the plan in a speech to the Consevative Party conference in the summer of 2020: "We know the United States is moving away from being the global guarantor of security and on the other side, China is challenging the balances which have kept us safe.

The policies outlined in the Integrated Review apply if either Trump or Biden wins the US election. The strategy applies whatever happens in India or China, or around the world.

We want to defend a loose network of alliances with countries which agree with our values and culture. Cooperation and partnership with France, Australia, Japan, India and Canada are especially important."

The trade war with China was one of the defining events of the Trump administration. But while in America, business and economic disagreements were at the root of the friction with China, for the United Kingdom, another matter was deemed extremely important: the fate of the former British colony of Hong Kong.

Following the expiry of a 99 year lease, Britain handed Hong Kong back to China in 1997. There was an understanding that the city would go on to enjoy a considerable degree of autonomy and run its affairs independently of the Chinese Communist Party, using a largely democratic political system. Particular emphasis was placed on the Sino-British Joint Declaration, signed in 1984 by a Chinese leader Zhao Ziyang, and Margaret

Thatcher. It was designed to be a lasting legacy of the revered Conservative prime minister.

By 2019, the democratic system in Hong Kong was under mounting pressure. Plans to extradite citizens to face trial in mainland China had provoked a wave of angry street protests. BBC television was on hand to capture the images. Viewers watched as young people chanted for democracy, often using English slogans or singing the refrains of Christian hymns. They protected themselves with yellow umbrellas as the police fired upon them with water cannons. To many, these plucky young people looked like courageous heroes. British MPs cheered them on from the House of Commons.

China emphasised that some of the protests had been violent and destructive. However, the British media tended to relay the anti-Chinese message of the protestors with enthusiasm. Editorials in the Economist, the Times and the Daily Telegraph, urged the British government to defend the principle of "one country, two systems" which gave Hong Kong its large degree of autonomy.

At one point in 2019, protesters daubed the Hong Kong parliament with graffiti and raised the former British colonial-era flag inside the building. This led to allegations by the Chinese authorities that foreign agents, including the British, were stirring up trouble. The response by China was severe. In the summer of 2020, new security laws were introduced which led to more than a hundred people being charged with sedition and terrorism. Many of them were high profile figures from the campaign for autonomy and democracy.

The British government responded with an unprecedented gesture. Hong Kong citizens with links to the UK were invited to apply for visas and move to Britain to start a new life. The

Chinese government once again complained that Britain was interfering in its internal affairs. The offer of the visas was seen as a politically bold move for the British government, as it came at a time when immigraion was a contentious issue in the UK.

Another important development in UK-China relations was the decision by the British government to ban Huawei from its 5G networks over security concerns, following pressure from America. The United States government warned that Huawei's equipment could potentially be used for spying and sabotage and imposed sanctions on the company. It expected the British to comply. As a result, in the summer of 2020, Boris Johnson's government announced it would ban the purchase of new kits made by Huawei for use in Britain's fifth-generation (5G) mobile networks. It followed advice from the British intelligence services that the American sanctions would make working with Huawei untenable.

The strong-arm tactics of the American therefore left the UK with little independence to choose the best way to deal with Huawei. Many commentators believed it was a clear example of the Americans pressing their allies to pick sides in their great power rivalry with China, in a way that had resonances to the Cold War with the USSR in the 1970s and 1980s.

In the context of Brexit, Boris Johnson sometimes seemed to want to take Britain out of the EU and yet also to retain many of the advantages of membership. A curious phrase entered the political vocabulary to describe this ambition. It was said the prime minister wanted "to have his cake and eat it". In other words, he somehow expected the cake to remain on the plate looking delicious, even after it had been consumed. This struck the EU side as an impossible fantasy.

A similar discrepancy appeared to be found in the approach to China. On the one hand, several of Britain's policies such as the banning of Huawei and the offer of visas to Hong Kong, riled the Chinese. However, the government also sought to "have its cake" with China in many other areas.

British consumers would enjoy cheap goods, imported from China. Many business links to China would continue, especially in the financial services industry. Tourists from mainland China would be encouraged to stay in hotels and visit attractions, such as the British Museum. And students from China would be welcome. The government would even let them live in the UK for two years after they graduated.

At the same time, many British universities developed well-resourced departments to teach China. A few professors with insight to the country became frequent press commentators and sometimes even advised the government.

Students who study the history of China in the 19th century always learn about the period when Britain invaded and occupied parts of the country, toward the end of its period of global colonial expansion. In China, this era, which includes the Opium Wars with Britain, is prominently included in the school curriculum. "Never forget our national shame," is a common message.

At press briefings in Beijing, spokespeople for China's Ministry of Foreign Affairs sometimes say that China should stand up proudly against the Western-colonialists who, in their view, are determined to hold back China's rise. There is anger that British warships are returning to the region, with American marines and weapons on their decks. Britain and the United States claim the navy is there to ensure freedom of navigation in the Indo-Pacific and to uphold a rules-based global order. But the Chinese Foreign Ministry repeats the view that historically, Britain has been a rule-breaker, an invader and a colonial power.

As other chapters in this book also make clear, Britain is not the only country resetting its relationship with China. The 21st century has also witnessed some significant changes in the tone of relations between China and the European Union. In 2021, the European Parliament spoke out against China on human rights issues in Xinjiang. China responded with sanctions, prompting the parliament to put on hold an investment deal with China.

As China has drawn more attention from the media, the public's opinion on it has changed. A survey undertaken by the Pew Research Centre in the summer of 2021 revealed widespread unfavourable views of China in many European countries.

Respondents showed little confidence in Xi Jinping's ability to handle foreign affairs and many people in Europe said they believed China had covered up the initial stages of the pandemic, to the detriment of the international effort to halt the spread of Covid-19. The survey suggested that people in Germany and France took a more negative view of China than citizens of the UK.

For China, these negative views do not seem to be provoking much concern. It sees no need to apologise to the British or the Europeans for its power and influence. Instead, under president Xi, there is a great deal of emphasis on the achievements of the Communist Party. Furthermore, a personality cult has grown around Mr Xi, who may well remain as China's leader for the rest of his life. State media never criticise him and there is heavy censorship of political views online.

In Britain and Europe, the media will not be quiet about China. Many MPs will also press their prime ministers to keep China near the top of their foreign affairs concerns. The pivot to Asia under Mr Johnson has set the direction of policy for future years. Of course, his successors may choose to change or reverse some of the plans. Nevertheless, leaders will still need to decide what form of relationship with China suits their own vision of global Britain.

(Duncan Bartlett is a Research Associate at the SOAS China Institute, where he presents the weekly podcast China in Context. He is also the Editor of Asian Affairs magazine).

Chapter 7
The Hong Kong-China Conflict: History Explained

– Estella C

Since the Handover in 1997, the Hong Kong-China relation has been strenuous. Following over a century of British rule, this small coastal city has taken a significantly different path, in terms of economically, politically and culturally, than its counterpart across the border.

The Sino-British Joint Declaration, signed by both China and the UK, grants Hong Kong a semi-autonomous status from China, separating it partially from the communist regime. The Basic Law, Hong Kong's own version of a mini-constitution, entails the "One Country, Two Systems" that has been causing controversies since.

"One Country, Two Systems" protects Hong Kong people's rights to protest, rally, demonstrate, assembly, and freedom of speech, all the rights abused in China. It is the guideline to structure the government and policies within the territory.

"Universal suffrage" is stated in the Basic Law as the ultimate goal for Hong Kong people. Currently, only a minority of 1,200 people who are considered to be the elites of society are eligible to elect the Chief Executive, the highest authoritative figure in the city. Universal suffrage means the candidates for the Chief Executive would be nominated by a broadly representative nominating committee. Hong Kong people feel they were promised a democracy that never came true, and it likely never will, thus resulting in a series of conflicts and anti-China protests in the next decades.

According to the Chinese constitution, its people are granted the rights of assembly, of demonstration, and freedom of speech. However, in reality, those rights are tightly monitored and controlled by the government. In Hong Kong, these rights are supposed to be valued and exercised.

Hong Kong is supposed to be given 50 years of autonomy after the Handover. The course has only gone half. Yet, China has taken increasingly aggressive measures to make the former British colony closer with the mainland in every aspect.

THE ANTI-CHINA EXTRADITION BILL PROTESTS

In February 2019, the Hong Kong government proposed the Fugitive Offenders and Mutual Legal Assistance in Criminal Matters Legislation (Amendment) Bill 2019, in response to the murder of a Hong Kong citizen by her boyfriend in Taiwan the year before. Citizens soon became concerned when the proposed bill included China, meaning the Hong Kong authority would have to hand over supposed fugitives under Chinese law.

One million people took to the streets to protest on June 9, according to the Civil Human Rights Front, the organiser. The number soon doubled to two million on June 16 for another protest march. The peaceful demonstration quickly escalated when tear gas and pepper spray were used by the police to deter protesters, marking the beginning of a long and volatile situation in the autonomous state.

China instantly took action in the land it claims to own historically to stop the spread of anti-China activities. Satellites captured tanks stationed in the Shenzhen Bay Sports Center, 5 kilometres away from the city border in early August 2019. At the time, critics speculated this was China's attempt to show Hong Kong and the world that "it was ready to use any force necessary to stop the riot". As the world watched on, most analysts believed China was merely bluffing rather than having the actual intention to use force.

Riot military response practice was also seen along the border. Police were practising tactics against rioters dressed in black with a yellow safety helmet, the same uniform used by protesters. Critics believed it was a direct warning from Beijing that it would do whatever it takes to put an end to the social instability.

Hong Kong is an important international financial hub. China has a lot at stake with billions of investments flowing between the borders. Dialling down the protest by military force would have raised international attention and traumatize the economy. China was walking on thin ice. One wrong step would only lead to a full-fledged revolution and a potential civil war, which the communist country was trying hard due to the worldwide media attention.

China's hope to deter protesters with its military showcase was proven to be unsuccessful. The protest that had gone on for 10 weeks showed no sign of slowing down. China's strong arm tactics did not seem to take effect.

Even after Chief Executive Carrie Lam withdrawn the bill, the protest went on. The focus of the protest was expanded to the demand for dual universal suffrage, the fundamental reason Hong Kong people are not satisfied with their home. They do not have to right to elect who gets to represent their rights, their interests, and their policies.

After a year of violent protests, the event gradually calmed down after many raids and arrests of political leaders, activists, and human rights organizations. Political activists sought asylum in countries like the US, the UK, and Taiwan.

Police brutality was a main concern during the protests. The media reported suspected Chinese army posing as Hong Kong riot police. Protesters claimed to have been raped and tortured in detention. Foreign journalists were also complaining to have been beaten up and shot by the police while covering the protests.

Hong Kong was once the safest city in Asia. Police brutality and abuse of power were rare, unlike in China, where it was happening often. Citizens were outraged to know that no police was sent to jail for the use of excessive force, which further posed a detrimental effect on the Hong Kong-China relationship.

THE NATIONAL SECURITY LAW THAT TOOK AWAY THE SECURITY OF HONG KONG PEOPLE

In June 2020, the Standing Committee of the National People's Congress enacted the Law of the People's Republic of China on Safeguarding National Security in the Hong Kong Special Administrative Region, also known as the Hong Kong National Security Law, in response to the months-long protests. The law criminalizes any act of secession, subversion, terrorism, and collusion with foreign forces.

The law received massive backlash locally and internationally with 27 countries voicing out their dismay and criticism against this unlawful act, which did not honour the Sino-British Joint Declaration. The absence of public consultation and full details of the law was a major concern. It was a rare occasion where the law's 66 articles were only released until after the law was enacted.

All of these crimes are punishable by a maximum sentence of life in prison. Beijing said the law is to restore order and stability to the society. Common protest tactics such as damaging public facilities are considered an act of terrorism.

China is using fear tactics to deter people's willingness to speak up. Under this law, mass gatherings traditionally held every June 4th and July 1st for the Tiananmen Massacre and the Handover would be forbidden. The Hong Kong government no longer allows protests and rallies on these historical event dates.

The National Security Law takes the Beijing law as the primary base. China follows constitutional law, as opposed to common law in Hong Kong. In case of any conflicts with the Hong Kong law, Beijing has the full power to interpret the terms. On top of that, the Chief Executive of Hong Kong has the power to appoint judges for cases under this law. Experts fear this will greatly undermine judicial autonomy in Hong Kong.

What's more worrying than the crumbling of the Hong Kong law system, is its impact on its economical status as an international financial centre. The law does not only apply to Hong Kong citizens but anyone on this land. It clearly states the inclusion of non-permanent residents as well as people from outside of the SAR who are not permanent residents of Hong Kong.

Economists expect a high volume of capital flowing out of the city as the concerns and distrust grow about the economic stability. The city has seen a high outflow of capital following the protests and the National Security Law. Residents are transferring billions of dollars of assets across the globe, mostly to English-speaking countries like Canada and the UK, with the hopes of starting a new life there as well.

THE NATIONAL SECURITY LAW AND APPLE DAILY

On 24 June 2021, the pro-democracy newspaper, Apple Daily, published its last issue, after being forced closed by Chief Executive Carrie Lam for breaching the National Security Law. A high-profile raid was conducted in its headquarter on 17 June 2021. Its founder and owner, Jimmy Lai, was arrested and more than $10 million in assets were ceased and frozen by the government. This was the first time a media company was forced to shut down following the controversial National Security Law. Citizens fear the city will soon completely lose its freedom of speech.

Named after the forbidden fruit, Apple Daily was founded by activist Lai in 1995. Being one of the few major media companies to be critical of China, this Cantonese newspaper became one of the best-selling publications in Hong Kong.

Apple Daily's strong stance against the government during the 2019 protests made it one of the most popular newspapers in Hong Kong. Officials appointed by China have blamed Apple Daily for instigating Hong Kong citizens to commit rioting and accused it of spreading false information harmful to national security.

Lai's advisor Mark Simmon informed the public that the hopes of Apple Daily coming back is slim. It would be a matter of time before it was closed. The original close date was set at 26 June. A day later, it was revised to be June 24.

The US president Joe Biden issued a statement in the White House, expressing concerns for the worrying situation threatening media freedom in Hong Kong and the tightened control of China. The statement called such action intensifies repression by Beijing against much-needed independent journalism.

By taking down its biggest critical media company, China is denying the basic freedom of speech the basic law grants Hong Kong. When the government can use national security as an excuse to annihilate the freedom of speech, media censorship is likely commonplace in the future. Citizens who are critical of China may face prosecution.

INFLUENCE UNDER THE NATIONAL SECURITY LAW

Government employees are required to sign or declare their allegiance to the Basic Law and the Hong Kong government since the last quarter of 2020. On 8 March 2021, the Secretary for the Civil Service Patrick Nip said nearly 200 civil servants refused to pledge their allegiance. He stated that the government would lose trust and faith in those who declined to vow their loyalty to the government and China and they would have to be let go.

Many civil servants voiced their support to the 2019 protests and organised campaigns and petitions for fellow civil servants to participate. This came in line with Beijing's plan for "patriots rule Hong Kong", where government employees should love and support China.

Freedom of speech is part of Hong Kong's core values. Civil servants should be offered a safe environment to voice out their criticism to the government for the betterment of society. They are at the forefront of the government. Beijing using the National Security Law as a reason to force civil servants to pledge their allegiance shows a firm determination to fully stop any forms of anti-government protests, thus limiting citizens' freedom to express their discontent.

Over the years, China has gotten into conflicts with the UK with its treatment of Hong Kong. Being an aggressively controlled society, China has continued to lose its popularity with Hong Kong people.

EXIT BAN THAT GIVES "UNFETTERED POWER" TO AUTHORITIES

Hong Kong amended its immigration law that would give the authorities the power to stop people from leaving the country, effective on August 1, 2021. Similar "exit bans" are common in China to stop political activists from leaving the country.

Although the government claimed the new law is aimed at curbing the influx of illegal asylum seekers, the new law gives absolute power to the immigration director to decide who cannot enter or exit Hong Kong. A court order is not required and there is no appeal system. The authority could easily abuse the system to stop political activists or persons of interest from leaving the territory.

The Hong Kong Bar Association (HKBA) said the bill would give the authority "apparently unfettered power". Even though the government stated the law only applies to flights coming into the semi-autonomous city, the unclear wording in the clause does not rule out the possibilities of the law being applied to those trying to leave Hong Kong, according to legal experts. The amendment sailed through the legislative council without opposition, again raising questions on how the law system reflects the will and interest of Hong Kong people.

ELECTION SCENE

The entire pro-democracy party resigned after four sitting legislators were disqualified following Beijing's new law for the disqualification of "unpatriotic" opposition legislators in early 2021.

Under the new law, anyone from the legislative council should not support the independence of Hong Kong, recognize the sovereignty of the Beijing regime, and should not commit any acts harmful to national security. Legislators failing to follow the rules will be barred from the council.

Mere hours after the new law was announced, the Hong Kong government immediately expulsed four legislators, causing outrage among other pro-democracy legislators and the public.

China has been tightening its control over Hong Kong since the enactment of the national security law. Such an attempt to clear out pro-democratic politicians severely limit the freedom and diversity in the legislative council.

Another grip the communist party has is the "Patriots Rule Hong Kong" scheme, which would significantly reduce the number of directly elected seats by half. Since the "reform" in the law-making body, a lot of policies and laws have been fast-tracked to approval and implementation, including the infamous "exit ban".

The future for the opposition camp is in the air. No one knows if they can ever come back, or if so, how. "Universal Suffrage" is far from realization for the people of Hong Kong. As China continues to tighten its grip politically, the city may soon descend to the same authoritarian leadership as its counterpart.

INTERNATIONAL RESPONSE

Canadian Prime Minister Justin Trudeau set up a special initiative for Hong Kong youth to move to Canada. The initiative allows Hong Kong citizens who graduated from a Canadian or overseas university in the last five years to stay and work in Canada for up to three years. Within the first three months, over 6,000 citizens sent in their applications.

The then-President Donald Trump passed the Hong Kong Human Rights and Democracy Act in November 2019 as a measure to oversee the "One Country, Two System" is being enforced and respected. The Act would lead to possible sanctions against those who committed human rights abuse in Hong Kong.

The UK introduced a scheme for all 3 million BNO passport holders in Hong Kong to live in the UK for five years, after which they will be eligible for citizenship. Other countries including Taiwan, the US, and Australia also have or in the process of introducing similar relaxed immigration policies for Hong Kong people.

China has condemned all of these countries for its attempts to help Hong Kong people, mostly accusing the countries to be interfering with its internal affairs.

THE FUTURE OF HONG KONG UNDER THE CHINESE RULE

After 24 years of turbulence and political instability, it is rather clear that Hong Kong will gradually lose all the freedom it was promised at the Handover way soon than in 1947. The rule of law in Hong Kong is being violated as the communist regime continues to force its rules and laws onto this harbour port.

The fight for universal suffrage and more freedom from China has been futile. When this 200-island archipelago was

Courtesy: dialoguechina.com

Chinese Naval Base Djibouti Courtesy Journal of Political Risk

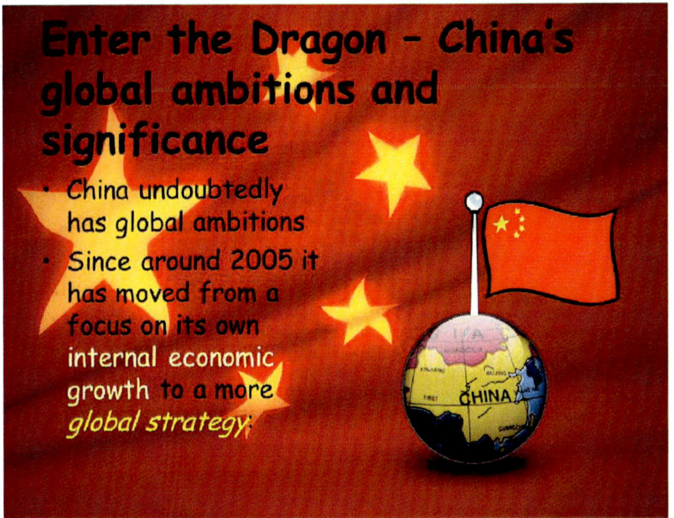

Courtesy South China Morning Post

China's Maritime Aggression Courtesy The Financial Express

China-Latin-America Courtesy Dialogo Chino

Belt and Road Initiative

Cracks in China-EU ties
Courtesy The Diplomat

BRI Courtesy LSEEMF

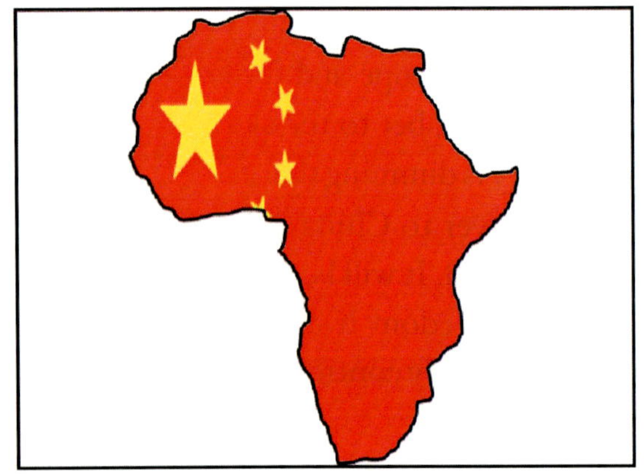

China in Africa Courtesy Orfonline.org

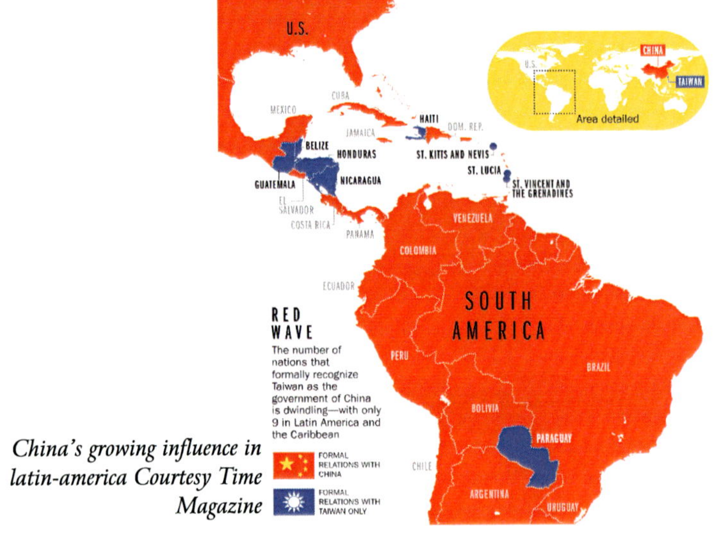

China's growing influence in latin-america Courtesy Time Magazine

Chinese Vaccine Diplomacy in Latin America Coutresy Xinhua

handed over to China, people saw hope and future to live the same life, dance to the same songs, bet to the same horse race, the dream to live in a free society is dimming sharp.

People's trust in the handover to China was based on the promises that were never delivered. It will be almost impossible for Hong Kong to regain the freedom it once had, let alone pursuing more, under the aggressively controlled Chinese rule.

(Estella C is a Sweden-based roving journalist and China analyst).

Chapter 8

Gazing at Tibet from Distant Beijing

– Gabriel Lafitte

How does China view Tibet, and the environment of the vast Tibetan Plateau?

China's perspective used to be straightforward, now no longer so, more a multi-fractal.

Until recently China viewed its empty quarter with horror and hope. Although occupying one quarter of China's territory, Tibet was largely defined by what it lacks: warmth, oxygen, cropland, population, cities, roads, modernity in any of its many manifestations. The only positives about this vast "waste land", as China called it, were its potential as a source of minerals, and the water of its rivers, especially the two that flow solely through China, the Yellow and Yangtze.

What long dominated revolutionary China's stance towards Tibet was its enormity, and China's tenuous hold on it. The Tibetan Plateau is 17 times the size of Bangladesh, or two thirds the size of India, but with only a tiny fraction of their population. For China, in the 1950s asserting actual control, for the first time, Tibet was a far frontier, and in many ways beyond the frontier, beyond the effective reach of a party-state seeking to turn the empire it inherited into a unitary nation-state.

Environment was off the agenda; if anything Tibet was altogether too natural, too forbidding, too remote, unnaturally frigid, its air dangerously thin, a land entirely unsuited to the intensive peasant cropping that had enabled China, over many centuries, to expand and expand.

Chinese scientific expeditions penetrated Tibet to map glaciers and minerals, to identify for the first time the sources of the great rivers that water most of Asia from Pakistan to Vietnam to northern China. The geologists were hailed as heroes, as shock troops of socialist construction, but actual exploitation of their many finds – chiefly copper, gold, molybdenum, boron, lithium and magnesium – was just too difficult, the sites too remote, too lacking in linkages to lowland China.

Mao's doctrine insisted that human will, under his direction, could conquer all obstacles, including nature. That meant "reclaiming waste land", by sending pastoralists into unpopulated alpine desert with their herds, to prove the triumph of the will. As elsewhere, the result was famine.

It was only decades later, well after Mao died, that China acknowledged its strategy in Tibet had largely failed, the forcible communisation of herds and herders in big communes had not worked. In the 1980s, China went to the opposite extreme, fragmenting pastoral society into individual households, each responsible for specific allocated and fenced winter pasture, almost always too small to maintain herd size in a land of unpredictable weather, extreme risks, and no social security, which meant the herd on the hoof was the only insurance against disaster.

Through Beijing's eyes the stubborn preference of pastoralists to maintain herd size, and kill as few animals as possible, was proof the nomads are irrational, selfish, ignorant and heedless of consequences. China applied its kisan logic to the innumerable plateaus spread across the open range, failing to understand the crucial role of nomadic mobility in maintaining grassland health.

Instead, China imposed carrying capacity constraints calculated in distant cities, imposing stocking rates that gradually drove the pastoralists into poverty and precarity, while failing to prevent overgrazing, erosion and degradation of allocated pastures. Demobilising nomads onto winter lands was bad for the soil, for productivity, income security and for China's hope to get more meat out of Tibet. Yet this foundational misunderstanding of how dryland pastoralism works has never been corrected. To this day China insists "there is a contradiction between grass and animals", which now requires many pastoralists to permanently leave their pastures, as the only way to grow more grass.

In this century, China has accelerated the removal of nomads, settling them on the fringes of new Chinese cities that cluster in zones of intensive extraction of oil, gas and lithium for making batteries; in mass tourism destinations; close by hydro dams. The policy of growing more grass by closing pastures – *tuimu huancao* – has intensified. This is because the northern China heartland of Han Chinese civilisation is now chronically short of water, and China sees Tibet as "China's Number One Water Tower." More grass protects more water flowing from the glacial sources over a thousand kilometres of alpine meadow, before dropping to the parched, industrialised, polluted lowlands.

This 21st century drive to rehabilitate land degradation, not by labour-intensive replanting but by excluding pastoralists from pastures, was the start of China reframing Tibet as an environmental policy issue.

China these days has much to say about environment, aiming to be accepted throughout the developing world as the model actor on environment, as well as the other issues that add up to comprehensive national power. China, the world's biggest polluter, faces great difficulties in positioning itself as a world leader on environment, and that is where its empty quarter enables it to play a positive role. Tibet is shifting, in Beijing's gaze, from a negative to a positive, from defining Tibet by what it lacks to championing it as national park and pristine wilderness. Lowland China is far too industrialised, populous and polluted to have much space for creating environmental credentials. But the underdeveloped Tibetan Plateau enables China to brand itself as dedicated protector of biodiversity, rivers and grasslands, with over 30 per cent of the plateau now designated as protected.

Does this mean the many countries downriver from Tibet can feel assured China will heed their need for clean waters and a clean environment? Does national park designation now protect Tibet's transboundary rivers from hydro damming, diversion and long-distance power grids? Does China's pledge to get to carbon neutrality protect Tibet and downstream countries from extremes of flood and drought? Are the areas in Tibet of maximum biodiversity now effectively protected? Will China's emissions trading scheme effectively cut carbon emissions? Is Tibet now protected from further industrialisation, urbanisation and agribusiness concentration of cattle herds, abattoirs and effluent pollution? Do the mines in Tibet do all that is needful to prevent waste tailings laden with toxic metals from entering the rivers?

These are questions India and Bangladesh should be asking, even though basic hydrological data on real time river flows are still state secrets.

Eastern India and Bangladesh are especially reliant on the Yarlung Tsangpo/Brahmaputra/Meghna river, which drains the entire north face of the Himalayas for over 2000 kms before cutting its way through the Himalayas to India. This makes China the upper riparian power, able with few constraints to fulfil its ambitions.

India is unused to recognising it is a lower riparian, with limited influence over what happens above, in Tibet, and no multilateral mechanism for consensual decision making or accountability. India has been well aware that in relation to both Pakistan and Bangladesh it is upper. Yet the Indus and Brahmaputra, as well as the Mekong of southeast Asia, the Salween of Myanmar and the Yangtze and Yellow Rivers of China all originate in Tibet.

From Beijing's perspective there is a big difference between the two rivers entirely within China, and the several trans-boundary rivers, which, once they leave China, are of little interest or concern. China has refused to join the Mekong River Commission or accept any formal commitment to multilateralism.

We are now in a time of intensive geostrategic competition between China and India along a Line of Control high in the Himalayas that bisects Tibet. Geostrategic tensions are fuelling China's ambition to assert its upper riparian power, and its occupation of the plateau high ground. Intensive militarization of the entire 3000 kms border is under way, including construction of hundreds of strategic border villages for power projection. Their hasty construction pays little heed to environmental concerns. Similarly, the stationing of heavy weaponry at high altitudes, backed by logistics hubs and fuel depots all pay no heed to environmental impacts.

China has many ambitions, some contradict others. China boasts it has already fulfilled the targets set by the UN Convention on Biodiversity seeking a proportion of national territory set aside for protecting biodiversity from threat of extinction. Yet China also has ambitious plans to speedily industrialise and urbanise much of Tibet, to intensify mining, hydro damming, power grid construction and the many dirty, heavy industries that process Tibetan minerals to sufficient purity to be used in lithium batteries, solar panels, copper wire and much more.

China wants enhanced flow of water from Tibet to its inland farmers and coastal factories, with hydroelectricity exported from Tibet across China to the world's factory. China wants the entire Tibetan Plateau zoned either as ecological or economic, which means the first 1000kms of the Yellow River are zoned ecological, then, still in Tibet, it becomes economic, exploited intensively for industry and aquaculture production of trout by the millions in the cold waters impounded in hydro dams.

China wants to make Tibet Chinese, part of nation-building narratives that erase Tibetan history and identity, including the deep cultural links between Tibet and India. Making Tibetan landscapes into Chinese landscapes means ongoing removal of herders and their herds, emptying the land of its traditional custodians, to be replaced by Chinese park administrators and tourism destination operators.

For people downstream, China's wide range of contradictory ambitions can be confusing. Yet some things remain constant. China has consistently viewed the Tibetans as a backward tribe, who need civilising, taught to become modern by the "orderly withdrawal" campaign to remove them from their lands, cancel their land tenure certificates, require them to sell all livestock, move to urban fringes and join the urban construction workforce.

Like upper riparians elsewhere, China relishes its advantageous positioning, and does not much care about its rivers once they leave Chinese territory, whether to India, Bangladesh, Pakistan, Myanmar, Lao, Thailand, Cambodia or Vietnam. China also excludes the Tibetan uppermost Mekong from its collaboration with the Asian Development Banks Greater Mekong Subregion (GMS) development program. Under GMS China plans to build highways and railways across Myanmar to link southern Chinese provinces with NE India, but these belt and road initiatives are currently halted by regional tensions.

Climate change in Tibet -the world's third pole- is accelerating fast, as at the other poles. As the glaciers melt river flow increases, a benefit China expects to persist for a few decades yet. As temperatures rise across Tibet, many lakes now brim over due to extra rain, floods are more frequent, triggering landslides and glacier lake dam outburst floods. Yet Chinese scientists see this as a long-term warming trend that makes Tibet more conducive to Chinese crops and Chinese settlement.

Climate change across the Tibetan Plateau has already reversed a trend of several millennia of the Indian monsoon shifting slowly eastward, leaving Tibet's far west increasingly dry. The monsoon is largely driven by the dramatic warming of the Tibetan Plateau in spring, as intense sunshine heats the bare rock of upper slopes. The heating is so intense it become the engine that pulls accumulating Indian Ocean and Bay of Bengal cloud cover deep inland, even through the gaps in the Himalayas. Now that dynamic is changing, the monsoon is becoming more erratic, yet from China's perspective all that matters is that a warmer and wetter climate in Tibet makes Tibet more like China, more conducive to Chinese ways.

While China highlights its environmental ambitions, it does not forego economic growth. That includes the West-to-East electricity transmission program, designed to knit Tibet firmly into China's world factory by exporting electricity from hydro dams on Tibetan rivers and from just below, over huge distances, all the way to China's coastal factories. Ongoing hydro dam construction is scheduled as part of China's 14th Five-Year Plan for 2021 through 2025, after a push by elite environmentalists to halt further dam building narrowly failed to become official policy.

The Five-Year Plan specifically mentions "the lower Yarlung Tsangpo" for further dam construction. From China's perspective, the lower Yarlung Tsangpo is roughly the 500 kms well downriver beyond Lhasa, but before the Yarlung Tsangpo enters India. That is a long stretch. From the viewpoint of hydro dam engineers, only a few locations are narrow enough to impound waters behind concrete walls that, in Tibet, are usually 300m high, yet not so high that access is difficult and the river so wild that construction is dangerous, even impossible.

A key question for India and Bangladesh is where any new dams on the "lower Yarlung Tsangpo" will be, and what impact they may have downstream. Armchair geostrategists have speculated that what China now plans to build is a dam that would dwarf even the Three Gorges Dam athwart the Yangtze, which is the world's biggest, and took over a decade to construct at vast expense. This speculation has understandably alarmed many in India and Bangladesh, since a dam collapse, whether accidental or an act of war, could cause enormous flooding downriver.

However, beyond the Five-Year Plan's vague mention of "lower Yarlung Tsangpo" there is almost no evidence of actual location, dam size, engineering feasibility, financing or preparatory activity in the great gorge of the Yarlung Tsangpo in its great southwards turn towards India.

Since the Himalayas continues to rise, the Yarlung Tsangpo continues to cut ever deeper, slicing right through the Eastern Himalayas, with adjacent mountains over 7000m on either side. The gorge is five kms deep, the deepest worldwide, and the Yarlung Tsangpo, confined to a narrow gorge even in the peak monsoon season, is a wild river. Perched far above are glaciers which, as global climate change warms the planet, have collapsed as recently as 2018, crashing millions of tons of mud, rock and ice all the way into the river below, so forcefully the entire river was halted, until it broke through again in a sudden rush, again causing great alarm down river.

Constructing a hydro dam in such an extreme landscape is beyond the capability even of China's hydro engineers. The landscape is too precipitous, too remote, too risky, too far from electricity demand, too prone to earthquakes and landslides, too inaccessible for massive turbines to be installed. In fact the turbines each weigh 500 tons or more, yet despite such weight are precision machinery to be emplaced in confined spaces with great accuracy; and a project of this magnitude would need a dozen or more turbines. Engineers have calculated that the only way to get such massive machinery to the site would be up river, through Bangladesh and NE India.

If it turns out that China is seriously planning a Great Bend mega dam, both Bangladesh and India have leverage, more than they might have imagined. You can't perch a crane kilometers above an almost vertical gorge and lower hundreds of tons of machinery into place from above, nor can the turbines be floated down a raging river.

In all likelihood, what China means by "lower Yarlung Tsangpo" is near Nyingtri, a fast growing tourist hill station on the route of the new Lhasa-Chengdu electrified rail line, all in need of more electricity. Geostrategists may consider this a security risk too, but not on the scale of the purported Great Bend mega dam.

China's ambitions are regional – the Belt and Road Initiative – and global. Many of the world's environmental problems are global, including climate change and the danger of losing many wildlife species.

China hopes to be an exemplary world leader on many fronts. Chinese manufacturers dominate global production of solar panels, wind turbines, lithium purification, long-distance ultra-high voltage electricity transmission, hydro dam construction, railway construction among many industries that are considered green alternatives to the present fossil fuelled economies of the world. China plans to dominate more of the new tech, and sees the Tibetan Plateau as its showroom to impress delegations from emerging economies.

However, when full life-cycle emergy assessments of these new technologies are done, they often have downsides, environmental impacts seldom mentioned, a more complex footprint than first imagined.

China makes bold statements about its environmental goals, such as establishing "the world's biggest emissions trading scheme" in July 2021. All 2200 coal fired power stations in China are required to participate. However, in practice this elaborate scheme puts only a nominal price on carbon, because permits to pollute continue to be given out freely. Tibetans in their customary role as custodians of landscapes that supply most of China's clean water, are in theory compensated for the ecosystem services they deliver, under emissions trading regimes. In reality, any revenue earned upriver, in Tibetan areas, goes not to the nomads but to local governments, to subsidise their removal of nomads.

On official figures, 40 million domestic tourists arrive in Lhasa every year, overwhelming a provincial capital with a population under ten lakhs. Now China is building airports all over Tibet, to cater to ever more arrivals, drawn by the prospect of virgin wilderness, often devoid of people or a Tibetan backstory. In the name of environment, carbon capture and water provisioning Tibetan pastoralists continue to be displaced form their landscapes, as if removal is the only path to achieving the environmental goal of rehabilitating degraded patches of soil.

China has never understood the logic of traditional Tibetan extensive land use and its strategy of moving on to prevent overgrazing. China continues to see itself as on a civilising mission to assimilate backward tribes, including the six million Tibetans, and to transform Tibetan landscapes into mass Chinese tourism destinations with Chinese signage, guides and characteristics.

For all these reasons the many countries below Tibet should look more closely at the adjacent uplands, and go beyond thinking of Tibet only as a geostrategic pawn in the great game of big power rivalry. Tibet matters to South Asia in many ways.

(Gabriel Lafitte is an Australian who has worked with Tibetans for over 40 years, publisher of a regular blog on Tibetan environmental issues, www.rukor.org, and author of several reports on Tibetan mineral extraction, development, nomads, climate change and wildlife.

Chapter 9

The South China Sea since the Arbitration: China's Growing Assertiveness

– Dr. Vo Xuan Vinh

For many years, China has increased its activities in the South China Sea to fulfill its ambition to monopolize the sea. China has repeatedly stated that its claims in the South China Sea are based on historical evidence, or historical rights. In fact, by the end of the first decade of the twentieth century, the southernmost latitude of China was only the Hainan Island.[1] In 1956, China occupied the Amphitrite Group of Paracel islands which was under the control of the South of Vietnam, and invaded and occupied the western portion of the Paracel Islands in 1974. In 1988, Chinese navy sank three Vietnamese ships, killing seventy-four sailors[2] and occupied Vietnam's occupied the reefs of Fiery Cross, Curteron, Gaven, Subi, and Hughes. In 1995, China occupied the Philippine-controlled Mischief.

On 7 May 2009, on pretext of objecting to Vietnam's Submission and Vietnam-Malaysia Joint Submission on the Outer Limit of the Continental Shelf, China sent the United

[1]See the Map in the Annex.

[2]China's Maritime Disputes 1895-2020, *Council on Foreign Relations*, https://www.cfr.org/timeline/chinas-maritime-disputes .

Nations Secretary General a diplomatic note attached by a map[3] stating its 'cow-tongue line'[4] or 'nine-dash line' or 'U-line'. This was the first time China officially circulated its U-line at international level.[5] After China seized the Scarborough Shoal and denied the Filipino's activities of fishing at and within 12 miles of the shoal in and after 2012,[6] the Philippines decided to bring China to Permanent Court of Arbitration (PCA) established under the Annex VII to the United Nations Convention on the Law of the Sea (UNCLOS). In July 12, 2016, the PCA issued its ruling in the high profile dispute between the Philippines and China which has been seen as the Philippines' historic victory over China[7] in the South China Sea. Although the arbitration has legal validity, there is no mechanism that can force China to implement the rulings so far.

After the PCA's rulings, China opposed the decision when it stated that the final award of the arbitration amounts to 'nothing more than a piece of paper' and China 'will never accept any solution imposed by a third party'[8] in one hand. In

[3]People's Republic of China, *Letter to the Secretary-General of the United Nations*. New York: The United Nations, May 07, 2009, http://www.un.org/depts/los/clcs_new/submissions_files/mysvnm33_09/chn_2009re_mys_vnm_e.pdf

[4]Diplomatic Academy of Vietnam (2012), *"Cow-Tongueline" – An Irrational Claim*. Hanoi: Tri Thuc Publishers, p.171.

[5]E. Frackx and M. Benatar, Dotted Lines in the South China Sea: Fishing for (Legal) Clarity, in Diplomatic Academy of Vietnam, *"Cow-Tongueline" – An Irrational Claim*. Hanoi: Tri Thuc Publishers, 2012, p.177.

[6]Permanent Court of Arbitration, *Hearing on Jurisdiction and Admissibility between the Republic of the Philippines and the People's Republic of China*, The Hague: Permanent Court of Arbitration, July 12, 2015, p.3.

[7]Carl Thayer, Who Decided the Philippines Versus China Case? *The Diplomat*, July 12, 2021, https://thediplomat.com/2021/07/who-decided-the-philippines-versus-china-case/

[8]Ministry of Foreign Affairs of the People's Republic of China, *Speech by Dai Bingguo at China-US Dialogue on South China Sea Between Chinese and US Think Tanks*, Washington D.C, July 5, 2016, https://www.fmprc.gov.cn/nanhai/eng/wjbxw_1/t1377747.htm

the other, China has continued to take more resolute activities to control the South China Sea such as increasing activities of reclamation, construction and militarization of its occupied features in the Spratlys, amending the Maritime Traffic Safety Law to allow its maritime law enforcement to act dangerously in the sea, further penetrating into other claimants' exclusive economic zones (EEZ), and increasing confrontation with the US.

By pointing out the absurdity of China's sovereignty claims based on the PCA's rulings, this chapter will evaluate the increase in China's actual control activities in the South China Sea after the award, and at the same time offer suggestions to limit China's illegal activities, partly contributing to maintaining peace, security and cooperation in the South China Sea.

CHINA'S CLAIM AND THE PCA'S RULINGS

China's claim in the South China Sea is based on the historical evidence, historical course or historical rights which has been protected under the United Nations Convention on the Law of the Sea (UNCLOS), as the Chinese officials stated. In Regular Press Conference on 15 September 2011, Chinese Foreign Ministry Spokesperson Jiang Yu asserted that 'China's claim on the South China Sea is grounded on sufficient historical and jurisprudential evidence'.[9] In Verbal CML 8/2011 dated 14 April 2011 sent to the Secretary-General of the United Nations, the Permanent Mission of the PRC to the UN stated that:

[9]Ministry of Foreign Affairs of the People's Republic of China, *Foreign Ministry Spokesperson Jiang Yu's Regular Press Conference on September 15, 2011*, http://www.china-embassy.org/eng/fyrth/t860126.htm

'China's sovereignty and related rights and jurisdiction in the South China Sea are supported by abundant historical and legal evidence'.[10]

In the 'Position Paper of the Government of the People's Republic of China on the Matter of Jurisdiction in the South China Sea Arbitration initiated by the Republic of the Philippines' released on 7 December 2014, the Ministry of Foreign Affairs of China stated that: 'China always maintains that the parties concerned shall seek proper ways and means of settlement through consultations and negotiations on the basis of respect for historical facts and international law'.[11] In 2015, in the Statement on the Award on Jurisdiction and Admissibility of the South China Sea Arbitration by the Arbitral Tribunal, Ministry of Foreign Affairs of the People's Republic of China highlighted that 'China's sovereignty and relevant rights in the South China Sea, formed in the long historical course', and "protected under international law including the United Nations Convention on the Law of the Sea (UNCLOS)."[12]

In 2012, China seized the Scarborough Shoal. The Philippines conducted a series of diplomatic activities to

[10]Note Verbale from the People's Republic of China to the Secretary-General of the United Nations, No. CML/8/2011 (14 April 2011), https://www.un.org/Depts/los/clcs_new/submissions_files/vnm37_09/chn_2011_re_phl_e.pdf

[11]Position Paper of the Government of the People's Republic of China on the Matter of Jurisdiction in the South China Sea Arbitration Initiated by the Republic of the Philippines,' 7 December 2014, https://www.fmprc.gov.cn/nanhai/eng/snhwtlcwj_1/t1368895.htm

[12]Statement of the Ministry of Foreign Affairs of the People's Republic of China on the Award on Jurisdiction and Admissibility of the South China Sea Arbitration by the Arbitral Tribunal Established at the Request of the Republic of the Philippines, October 30, 2015, https://www.fmprc.gov.cn/mfa_eng/zxxx_662805/t1310474.shtml.

demand Chinese to withdraw from the shoal but the latter remained their presence there as well as denying the Filipino's activities of fishing at and within 12 miles of the shoal, the Philippines brought China to the PCA. In the PCA's rulings issued in July 12, 2016, China's claim was refuted.

Regarding China's sovereign claim in the scope of 'nine-dash line' in the South China Sea, the PCA awarded that:

> 'China has never expressly clarified the nature or scope of its claimed historic rights. Nor has it ever clarified its understanding of the meaning of the 'nine-dash line'.[13]

and

> 'the Tribunal understands that China claims rights to the living and non-living resources within the 'nine-dash line', but (apart from the territorial sea generated by any islands) does not consider that those waters form part of its territorial sea or internal waters'.[14]

> 'The Tribunal is unable to identify any evidence that would suggest that China historically regulated or controlled fishing in the South China Sea, beyond the limits of the territorial sea'.[15]

Regarding China's claim that grounded on 'historic rights' or 'historic course', the Tribunal judged that:

> 'The Convention does not include any express provisions preserving or protecting historic rights that are at variance with the Convention. On the contrary, the Convention

[13]Permanent Court of Arbitration (2016), *PCA Case Nº 2013-19 in the Matter of the South China Sea Arbitration between the Republic of the Philippines and the People's Republic of China*, The Hague: Permanent Court of Arbitration, July 12, p.71.

[14]Permanent Court of Arbitration, op.cit., pp.91-92.

[15]Permanent Court of Arbitration, op.cit., p.114.

supersedes earlier rights and agreements to the extent of any incompatibility. The Convention is comprehensive in setting out the nature of the exclusive economic zone and continental shelf and the rights of other States within those zones. China's claim to historic rights is not compatible with these provisions'.[16]

The Tribunal further explained:

The term 'historic rights' is general in nature and can describe any rights that a State may possess that would not normally arise under the general rules of international law, absent particular historical circumstances. Historic rights may include sovereignty, but may equally include more limited rights, such as fishing rights or rights of access, that fall well short of a claim of sovereignty'.[17]

The Tribunal also added:

'Accordingly, upon China's accession to the Convention and its entry into force, any historic rights that China may have had to the living and non-living resources within the 'nine-dash line' were superseded, as a matter of law and as between the Philippines and China, by the limits of the maritime zones provided for by the Convention'.[18]

Therefore,

'the Tribunal concludes that China's claim to historic rights to the living and non-living resources within the 'nine-dash line' is incompatible with the Convention to the extent that it exceeds the limits of China's maritime zones as provided for by the Convention'.[19]

[16]Permanent Court of Arbitration, op.cit., p.103.

[17]Permanent Court of Arbitration, op.cit., p.96.

[18]Permanent Court of Arbitration, op.cit., p.111.

[19]Permanent Court of Arbitration, op.cit., p.111.

Regarding China's claim grounded on historic rights or sovereign rights in the scope of 'nine-dash line',

> 'the Tribunal concludes that, as between the Philippines and China, China's claims to historic rights, or other sovereign rights or jurisdiction, with respect to the maritime areas of the South China Sea encompassed by the relevant part of the 'nine-dash line' are contrary to the Convention and without lawful effect to the extent that they exceed the geographic and substantive limits of China's maritime entitlements under the Convention. The Tribunal concludes that the Convention superseded any historic rights or other sovereign rights or jurisdiction in excess of the limits imposed therein'.[20]

In short, China's claim in the South China Sea which bases on 'historic rights' or 'historic course' was rejected by the PCA's rulings on July 12, 2016. In other words, 'the tribunal concluded that the Chinese territorial claim in the South China Sea has no legal basis'.[21]

CHINESE GROWING ASSERTIVENESS

Growing Reclamation, Construction and Militarization

Since the beginning of 2014, the international press has widely reported that China has been conducting land reclamation and construction on six of its seven occupied features in the Spratlys in the South China Sea, transforming the submerged reefs and rocks into full-pledged islands with airstrips, harbors and other

[20]Permanent Court of Arbitration, op.cit., p.117.

[21]Abhay Kumar Singh, South China Sea Conundrum- Plus ça change, in M.S. Prathibha, *China's Rising Strategic Ambitions in Asia*, New Delhi, Pentagon Press, 2018, p.87.

military and civilian structures.[22] In fact, China's reclamation work in the Spratly Island appears to have begun as early as September 2013.[23] According to information released in August 2015 by Pentagon:

> Since Chinese land reclamation efforts began in December 2013, China, ... as of June 2015, had reclaimed more than 2,900 acres of land. By comparison, Vietnam has reclaimed a total of approximately 80 acres; Malaysia, 70 acres; the Philippines, 14 acres; and Taiwan, 8 acres. China has now reclaimed 17 times more land in 20 months than the other claimants combined over the past 40 years, accounting for approximately 95 percent of all reclaimed land in the Spratly Islands.[24]

China has created artificial islands of most of its occupied features in the South China Sea. There are seven reclamations in the Spratly islands and twenty in Paracel islands.[25] At the press conference held by the third Session of the Chinese twelfth National People's Congress on March 8, 2015, China for the first time officially confirmed its activities of reclamation and construction.[26] A month later, the purposes of the move were

[22]Tran Truong Thuy, Vietnam's Maritime Security Challenges and Responses, in The National Institute for Defense Studies (Japan), Security Outlook of the Asia Pacific Countries and Its Implications for the Defense Sector, *NIDS Joint Research Series* No. 13, 2015, p.87.

[23]Ben Dolven et al., Chinese Land Reclamation in the South China Sea: Implications and Policy Options, *CRS Report*, June 18, 2015, p.13

[24]Department of Defense, *Asia-Pacific Maritime Security Strategy*, 2015, p.16.

[25]Amruta Karambelkar, 'Chinas Militarisation of South China Sea, *Vivekananda International Foundation*, September 15, 2020, https://www.vifindia.org/2020/september/15/china-s-militarisation-of-south-china-sea.

[26]Ministry of Foreign Affairs of the People's Republic of China, *Foreign Minister Wang Yi Meets the Press*, 2015/03/08, http://www.fmprc.gov.cn/mfa_eng/zxxx_662805/t1243662.shtml

listed by Chinese Foreign Ministry spokesperson Hua Chunying on April 9, 2015 as 'optimizing' the functions of islands and reefs, 'improving the living and working conditions of personnel stationed there', 'better safeguarding territorial sovereignty and maritime rights and interests', 'better performing China's international responsibility', and 'satisfying the need of necessary military defense'.[27]

For the purpose of military defense, China has enhanced militarization in the South China Sea. In February 2016, China has deployed surface-to-air missile systems and then sent Shenyang J-11 and Xian JH-7 fighter jets[28] on Woody Island in the Paracel Islands which China used force to occupy from Vietnam in 1956 and 1974 respectively. With a range of 120 miles and an ability to hit moving air targets at a height of 90,000 feet, China's air defence missile systems on the island has become a threat to regional security environment. In the same month, China deployed fighter jets to Woody Island. China was also reported to have installed a high frequency radar on Cuarteron reef in the Spratly islands.[29] In 2018, China continued the militarization in the South China Sea by placing anti-ship cruise missiles and long-range surface-to-air missiles on outposts in the Spratly Islands, violating a 2015 pledge by

[27]Ministry of Foreign Affairs (The People's Republic of China), *Foreign Ministry Spokesperson Hua Chunying's Regular Press Conference on April 9, 2015*, 2015/04/09, http://www.fmprc.gov.cn/mfa_eng/xwfw_665399/s2510_665401/t1253488.shtml

[28]China sends fighter jets to contested island in South China Sea: Fox News, *Asia Times*, February 23, 2016, http://atimes.com/2016/02/china-sends-fighter-jets-to-contested-island-in-south-china-sea-fox-news/

[29]China building radar on Spratly isles, *The Star Online*, February 24, 2016, http://www.thestar.com.my/news/regional/2016/02/24/china-building-radar-on-spratly-isles-installation-would-significantly-change-the-operational-landsc/

Chinese President Xi Jinping that "China does not intend to pursue militarization" of the Spratly Islands.[30] The presence of China's anti-ship cruise missiles and long-range surface-to-air missiles on outposts in the Spratly Islands have given China certain advantages since it could create the deterrence capacity located in the centre of the South China Sea.

Revision on Maritime Traffic Safety Law

After the PCA issued the decision only several months, in November 2016, the Chinese Standing Committee of the National People's Congress passed the decision to amend the 1984 Maritime Traffic Safety Law. In February 2017, the Committee announced that it is soliciting public opinions on the revisions to the law. In April 2021, the Committee voted in favor of an amended Maritime Traffic Safety Law, which will take effect in September 01, 2021.

Under the new rules, which expand the authority of the Maritime Safety Administration, foreign ships found to be potentially hazardous to marine traffic safety will be required to report themselves before sailing through the so-called Chinese waters. Ships found in violation will be ordered to vacate. Violators are subject to fines between 50,000 Yuan and 500,000 Yuan (US$7,700 to US$77,000).[31] Especially, according to the new amended law, the Chinese coast guard is allowed to use "all necessary means", including firing on foreign vessels, to stop or

[30]Office of the Secretary of Defense, Military and Security Developments Involving the People's Republic of China 2019, *Annual Report to Congress*, May 2019, p.ii.

[31]Tsukasa Hadano, China's new maritime law fines ships that violate its waters, *Nikkei Asia*, 30 April 2021, https://asia.nikkei.com/Politics/International-relations/Indo-Pacific/China-s-new-maritime-law-fines-ships-that-violate-its-waters.

prevent threats from foreign vessels. The law allows coast guard personnel to demolish other countries' structures built on Chinese-claimed reefs and to board and inspect foreign vessels in waters claimed by China. It also empowers the coastguard to create temporary exclusion zones "as needed" to stop other vessels and personnel from entering.[32] With the move, Chinese authority is trying to legitimize its law enforcement force in the South China Sea. The move also creates potential of conflict which in turn jeopardize the safety of SLOC within the sea.[33]

Growing Penetration into the EEZs of other Claimants

After the arbitration, China has increased activities in the South China Sea, especially the penetration into the EEZs of other claimants. In the case of Vietnam, in the beginning of July, 2019, Chinese survey ship Haiyang Dizhi 8 entered waters northeast of Vanguard Bank in the South China Sea to conduct seismic survey. It was escorted by over 20 Chinese coast guard vessels[34] and Vietnamese coast guard confronted it resulting in a stand-off between them. Apparently, the purpose of Chinese survey ship was to obstruct Vietnam's survey activity where a Japanese offshore rig, Hakuryu 5 was drilling for Russia's Rosneft Vietnam in block 6.1 since May 2019. The area is also close to where

[32]Yew Lun Tian, China authorises coast guard to fire on foreign vessels if needed, *Reuters*, January 22, 2021, https://www.reuters.com/article/us-china-coastguard-law-idUSKBN29R1ER

[33]Abhay Kumar Singh, "South China Sea Conundrum- Plus ça change", in M.S. Prathibha, *China's Rising Strategic Ambitions in Asia*, New Delhi, Pentagon Press, 2018, p.92.

[34]Dipanjan Roy Chaudhury, Vietnam justified in defending its rights in Vanguard Bank in South China Sea, *The Economic Times*, September 30, 2019, https://economictimes.indiatimes.com/news/defence/vietnam-justified-in-defending-its-rights-in-vanguard-bank-in-south-china-sea/articleshow/71368439.cms?from=mdr

national oil company PetroVietnam and Mubadala Development of the United Arab Emirates' were jointly exploring Block 136-03. It is important to note that Vanguard Bank is the western most reef of the Spratly Island and is located within 200 nautical miles of Vietnam's EEZ off Hai islet (Phu Quy group). Similarly, Block 6.1 is in Vietnamese EEZ off provinces of Tra Vinh or Phan Thiet of Vietnam. In response to Chinese's activities in Vietnam's EEZ and continental shelf, the United States on 22 August 2019 expressed its deeply concerned that 'China is continuing its interference with Vietnam's longstanding oil and gas activities in Vietnam's Exclusive Economic Zone (EEZ) claim'.[35] On 26 September 2019, the U.K., France and Germany released a joint statement in which three countries call on 'all coastal states of the South China Sea to take steps and measures that reduce tensions and contribute to maintaining and promoting peace, security, stability and safety in the region, including as regards the rights of coastal states in their waters' and urged that the legal framework set out by the United Nations Convention on the Law of the Sea granting several claimants sovereign rights to the waters 'must be carried out'.[36]

In October 2019, the West Capella, a drillship operated by London-managed Seadrill and contracted to Petronas, began operating in oil and gas block ND4 off the coast of Malaysia's Sabah State. From December 6 to 9, two Chinese Coast Guard

[35]US Department of State, *China Escalates Coercion against Vietnam's Longstanding Oil and Gas Activity in the South China Sea*, Press Statement, August 22, 2019, https://www.state.gov/china-escalates-coercion-against-vietnams-longstanding-oil-and-gas-activity-in-the-south-china-sea/

[36]Philip Heijmans, U.K., France, Germany 'Concerned' About South China Sea Tensions, *Bloomberg*, August 30, 2019, https://www.bloomberg.com/news/articles/2019-08-30/uk-france-germany-concerned-about-south-china-sea-tensions.

(CCG) ships – the Haijing 5202 and 5403 – patrolled around the vessel. On December 21, 2019, the West Capella moved to block ND2 an area which both Malaysia and Vietnam claim as part of their extended continental shelves in the South China Sea. The CCG responded almost immediately when in the same day, the 5202 again detoured from its duties escorting Chinese fishing vessels in the area to patrol around the West Capella. A day later, China dispatched the Haijing 5203 from Hainan to Luconia Shoals. For the next two months, the *Zhaojun*-class 5203 split its time between harassing the West Capella and intimidating oil and gas operations closer to Luconia Shoals.[37] In April 2020, a Chinese government survey ship, Haiyang Dizhi 8, tagged the West Capella, an exploration vessel operated by Malaysia's state oil company Petronas. Haiyang Dizhi 8 was flanked at one point by more than 10 Chinese vessels, including those belonging to maritime militia and the coast guard. The ship was 324 km (200 miles) off the Malaysian coast, within Malaysia's EEZ.[38] Asian Maritime Transparency Initiative (AMTI) showed that since December 2019 to May 2020, Chinese fishing vessels have operated near the West Capella while CCG ships continued to harass the rig and its supply vessels. In response, Malaysian navy and law enforcement ships have been regularly patrolling the area.[39]

[37]Malaysia picks three way fight in the South China Sea, *Asia Maritime Transparency Initiative*, February 21, 2020, https://amti.csis.org/malaysia-picks-a-three-way-fight-in-the-south-china-sea/

[38]A. Ananthalakshmi, Rozanna Latiff, Chinese and Malaysian ships in South China Sea standoff: sources, *Reuters*, April 17, 2020, https://www.reuters.com/article/us-malaysia-china-southchinasea/chinese-and-malaysian-ships-in-south-china-sea-standoff-sources-idUSKBN21Z1TN.

[39]Chinese Survey Ship Escalates Three-Way Standoff, *Asia Maritime Transparency Initiative*, May 18, 2020, https://amti.csis.org/chinese-survey-ship-escalates-three-way-standoff/

In the case of the Philippines, in the end of May 2021, it was stated that the administration of Philippine President Rodrigo Duterte has filed 100 diplomatic protests against China's various incursions in the South China Sea. The incursions were described by the Philippine side as incessant deployment, prolonged presence, and illegal activities of Chinese vessels. Since April 2021, hundreds of Chinese boats were spotted last month at the boomerang-shaped Whitsun Reef in the Spratly Islands, the Philippines has been filing protests almost daily.[40]

Continuity of Actions Challenging the U.S.

If in December 2013, the US guided missile warship USS Cowpens was challenged when it was conducting surveillance of China's new aircraft carrier, the Liaoning in the South China Sea. The incident happened in October 2018 seemed to be a Chinese harder challenge to the U.S. It seemed that China was more proactive in challenging the US military presence in the South China Sea. On September 30, 2018, the U.S. Navy destroyer USS Decatur had to maneuver to avoid a collision after the Chinese warship Luyang came within 45 yards of its bow as the American ship transited in the vicinity of Gaven Reef in the South China Sea.

WHAT SHOULD BE DONE?

In order to settle the dispute in the South China Sea, there are some possibilities that we could think about. China's self-

[40] 100 protests filed against China's incursions in Philippine waters, *The Straits Times*, May 31, 2021, https://www.straitstimes.com/asia/se-asia/over-100-protests-filed-against-chinas-incursions-in-philippine-waters-dept-of-foreign.

restraint and upholding of international law are the best option for all. China has 'reaffirmed the importance of maintaining and promoting peace, security, stability, safety and freedom of navigation in and over-flight above the South China Sea', 'the importance of upholding international law, including the 1982 UNCLOS', 'pursue peaceful resolution of disputes in accordance with the universally recognized principles of international law, including the 1982 UNCLOS'.[41] However, China's objection to the 2016 PCA's rulings and its growing assertiveness in the South China Sea show that China has not and will not obey the international law, including the 1982 UNCLOS. It is unrealistic to think about China's self-restraint and upholding of international law in dealing with the South China Sea dispute.

Another factor hoped to deal with the situation is ASEAN. ASEAN issued the first declaration on the South China Sea in 1992 and its member states have been making efforts to realize a Code of Conduct (COC) in the South China Sea to replace the non-binding Declaration on the Conduct of Parties in the South China Sea (DOC) released in 2002 between ASEAN member states (AMS) and China. AMSs have also reaffirmed that the 1982 UNCLOS is the basis for determining maritime entitlements, sovereign rights, jurisdiction and legitimate interests over maritime zones, and the 1982 UNCLOS sets out the legal framework within which all activities in the oceans and seas must be carried out.[42] However, ASEAN's decisions are based on consensus and only four out of ten AMSs are claimants

[41] *Chairman's Statement of the 23rd ASEAN-China Summit*, November 12, 2020, https://asean.org/storage/47-Final-Chairmans-Statement-of-the-23rd-ASEAN-China-Summit.pdf

[42] *Chairman's Statement of the 37th ASEAN Summit*, November 12, 2020, https://asean.org/storage/43-Chairmans-Statement-of-37th-ASEAN-Summit-FINAL.pdf

in the South China Sea. During the process of COC negotiations between AMSs and China, it seems that only some claimants have been seeking for a legally binding COC when others do not want. In other words, AMSs do not speak the same voice regarding the South China Sea dispute. ASEAN is not a united group in dealing the South China Sea issue with China.

Against that background, there should be a realistic approach in dealing with the South China Sea dispute. China's ambition is to monopolize the South China Sea. AMSs as claimants themselves should upgrade capacity to protect their sovereignty and other legitimate interests in the South China Sea while ASEAN as a group should continue their commitments as they have been doing regarding the issue. Countries outside the regions such as the U.S., Japan, Australia, India, Canada, the U.K., France, and Germany should protect their legitimate interests, including freedom of navigation, overflights, and unimpeded trade in the South China Sea. The said countries could treat China in a hard way (deterrence) to force the latter to behave in accordance with universal recognized principles of international law, including UNCLOS 1982, with China as a party, in the South China Sea.

CONCLUSION

China has a process of forcefully occupying and invading the South China Sea. After the PCA's rulings concluded that China's territorial claim in the South China Sea is illegal, China has even increased its assertiveness by, among others, continuing of reclamation, construction and militarization; revising domestic law to allow it maritime law enforcement to act more dangerously, if needed; and growing penetration into EEZs of other claimants; and stronger challenging to the U.S. China's growing assertiveness in the South China Sea has further increased tension, violated other claimants' sovereignty and their other legitimate interests in the sea. China's assertiveness has also challenge countries outside the region which have interests in, among others, freedom of navigation, over-flight and unimpeded trade. In that context, a hard approach, i.e. the deterrence, conducted by countries having interests in the region such as the U.S., Japan, Australia, India, Canada, the U.K., France, and Germany to protect universally recognized principles of international law, including the 1982 UNCLOS, is needed.

(Dr. Vo Xuan Vinh is with the Institute for Southeast Asian Studies Vietnam Academy of Social Sciences, Hanoi.)

Annex:

The complete map of the Qing Empire (1908)

大清帝國, 大清帝國全圖, 宣統元年,上海商務印書館, 1908.
The complete map of the Qing Empire, Shanghai Commercial Press, 1908.

Chapter 10

China's Global Ambitions: US Perspectives and Responses

– Michael Kugelman

(This essay[1] offers a US perspective on China's foreign policy objectives, and it examines Washington's policy responses during the Trump era and the first part of the Biden administration. It also offers a vision for how Washington can best manage China's rise).

In hyperpoliticized Washington, just about everything is polarizing and partisan—including foreign policy. While there are exceptions—including buy-in from both major political parties for deepening U.S.-India partnership, supporting Israel, and fighting Islamist terror—most foreign policy issues don't enjoy bipartisan backing and are politically divisive.

This politicization of foreign policy is not new in America. It has long been the case for issues such as climate change, and policy toward Cuba and Iran. It has also traditionally been the case for arguably the most consequential contemporary U.S. foreign policy concern: The rise of China.

For many years, there was disagreement among U.S. policymakers, analysts, and academics about what Beijing aims

[1]This chapter is based in part on Michael Kugelman, "U.S. China Policy: Roots, Ramifications, and Responses," *World Focus* (October 2020).

to gain from its rise. Some took a hawkish position, believing that China sought to become a military superpower and that its growing power posed a major threat to U.S. interests. Others espoused a more sanguine view, arguing that Beijing's growth was largely economic, and that it should be treated as a partner, not a pariah.

However, ever since President Xi Jinping assumed power in 2013, a strong consensus has been emerging within U.S. policy circles, and within the broader American intellectual and political elite, that China's global ambitions pose a threat to U.S. interests—and to America's 30-year status as the world's sole superpower. Not surprisingly, another longtime policy disagreement in America about China—how to respond to its rise—is melting away in favor of a new consensus: One that favors countering China, not engaging it.

The Wolf Warrior Eclipses the Dragon

The government of China, like that of many countries in recent years, is deeply nationalistic. The strong undercurrents of nationalism in its foreign policy are best reflected in "wolf warrior diplomacy," a term used to describe its current muscular foreign policy.[2] This entails acting assertively—many in Washington would say aggressively—to deepen its global footprint and to pursue its interests overseas. This foreign policy is pursued on five different fronts—all of which concern Washington, to varying degrees.

The first is economic—perhaps the most visible and frequent manifestation of China's deepening global footprint.

[2]See Zhiqun Zhu, "Interpreting China's 'Wolf-Warrior Diplomacy'," *The Diplomat*, May 25, 2020, https://thediplomat.com/2020/05/interpreting-chinas-wolf-warrior-diplomacy/.

Beijing's investment imprint extends to the world's farthest reaches, and ranges from large-scale agricultural land acquisitions to port development, and so much in between. The chief vehicle for furthering Chinese economic clout is the Belt and Road Initiative (BRI).[3]

Washington's anxieties are not about Chinese economic investment per se; the basic objectives of Beijing's infrastructure projects—creating more employment, growth, prosperity, and stability—align well with U.S. interests in the developing world, a key locus for Chinese investment. Rather, Washington worries about the nature of these investments, which it believes to be opaque and even predatory. One of the most comprehensive U.S. critiques of Chinese investments came from a speech by Ambassador Alice Wells, then the senior U.S. State Department official for South Asia, in 2019.[4]

And yet, what's even more problematic for Washington is that China's investment footprint is especially deep in areas that U.S. policymakers consider to be highly strategic, but where America is much less popular and present than is China. Pakistan and Central Asia are two notable examples.

China's second foreign policy front is diplomatic. Put simply, Beijing is casting as wide a diplomatic net as possible to increase its power. It is deepening relations with as many countries as possible. It is riding on the coattails of its infrastructure

[3]The American Enterprise Institute's Global Investment Tracker, which estimates over $2 trillion in Chinese global investment since 2005, provides useful data. See https://www.aei.org/china-global-investment-tracker/.

[4]"A Conversation with Alice Wells on the China-Pakistan Economic Corridor," the Wilson Center, November 21, 2019, https://2017-2021.state.gov/a-conversation-with-ambassador-alice-wells-on-the-china-pakistan-economic-corridor/index.html.

investments, in that it is strengthening diplomatic relations with the countries where it is deploying capital. One of the major consequences of this diplomatic push is more competition with India, its biggest regional rival. Beijing has brought both BRI and better relations to Bangladesh, Maldives, Nepal, and Sri Lanka—all countries that have historically close ties to India. For Washington, which views New Delhi as its best strategic bet for pushing back against Beijing's growing clout in Asia, this is bad news.

However, China's coupling of investment and diplomatic engagement risks backfiring. Beijing arguably gains diplomatic leverage over the largely poor, developing countries in which it is investing through the debt they incur from Chinese loans. But this leverage—which some experts call "debt trap diplomacy"—could be undercut if this financial dependence on China prompts public anger and compels governments to take on less Chinese financing.[5]

At any rate, Beijing's diplomatic outreach extends far beyond the countries where it is investing. It is taking on prominent roles in the world's emerging multilateral groupings — such as the Asian Infrastructure Investment Bank, where it is the largest stakeholder—and in influential regional groupings, such as the Shanghai Cooperation Organization. It's also

[5]Indian strategic analyst Brahma Chellaney is credited with coining the term "debt trap diplomacy." See Brahma Chellaney, "China's Debt-Trap Diplomacy," *Project Syndicate*, January 23, 2017, https://www.project-syndicate.org/commentary/china-one-belt-one-road-loans-debt-by-brahma-chellaney-2017-01. Some scholars, however, reject the idea of debt trap diplomacy. See Deborah Brautigam and Meg Rithmire, "There is No Chinese 'Debt Trap," *The Atlantic*, February 6, 2021, https://www.theatlantic.com/international/archive/2021/02/china-debt-trap-diplomacy/617953/.

deepening ties with America's top rivals (Iran, Russia) and with some of its most difficult partners (Pakistan, Turkey).

China's third foreign policy front is cultural: The export of its values, customs, cuisine, and more—in other words, soft power. Seen at face value, China's tremendous soft power should not be concerning for the United States—especially given the longstanding cultural relations between the two countries, the major impact of Chinese culture (from cuisine to language and film) on American life, and the existence of the Chinese diaspora in America, one of the country's largest.

However, many in the United States view the projection of Chinese soft power as a reflection of, if not a proxy for, its growing global footprint. In countries like Nepal, for example—where until relatively recent India, not China, was the most influential foreign player—Beijing has sought to cultivate clout not just through infrastructure investments, but through the encouragement of Chinese language classes, among other things.[6] In 2021, during the coronavirus pandemic, Beijing used a new tool—vaccine exports—to strengthen its soft power. This tactic enabled China to gain another upper hand in its strategic rivalry with India, which launched its own vaccine diplomacy campaign in South Asia earlier in 2021, before a devastating surge of COVID-19 compelled it to halt exports.

Additionally, many Americans believe that Beijing leverages its soft power to mask Chinese wrongdoing. In 2020, Disney filmed a live-action version of the animated classic "Mulan" in the Chinese province of Xinjiang. The film's end credits thanked government officials and agencies in the province. This sparked

[6]Sahitya Ratna Rana, "China's Soft Power Through Higher Education in Nepal," FINS, July 13, 2021, https://finsindia.org/dragons-soft-power-through-higher-education-in-nepal/.

an uproar in the United States, given that it is in Xinjiang where officials have committed gross human rights abuses against the Uighur Muslim community.[7]

China's fourth foreign policy front is technological. It seeks to deploy this capacity abroad through trade and investment. Beijing's global technology presence is huge, thanks to large telecommunications firms like Huawei. However, Washington and many Americans perceive Chinese technology as a threat because of surveillance risks. U.S. officials also believe China is behind cyber attacks on America. While the Biden administration has sought cooperation with Russia—another country that America accuses of hacking—on promoting cyber security, its position toward China—at least during the early part of its term—has appeared more confrontational.

China's fifth foreign policy pillar is military—arguably the one of most concern for Washington. For years, it has been undertaking rapid military modernization to better enable it to project sea, air, and land power. This is in of itself a concern for the United States, given that China—by virtue of its size and economic and military strength—is America's top strategic competitor. Additionally, there is bipartisan concern in Washington about the increasingly muscular use of Chinese military power—and especially because this military power often threatens the interests of top U.S. partners. Its maneuvers in the South China Sea directly impact U.S. Asian treaty allies. It is attempting to impose its will in Hong Kong and Taiwan, two important but vulnerable U.S. friends. And its border provocations against India—first in the Doklam Plateau and

[7]Amy Qin and Edward Wong, "Disney's 'Mulan' Criticized for Filming in Xinjiang," *The New York Times*, September 8, 2020, https://www.nytimes.com/2020/09/08/world/asia/china-mulan-xinjiang.html.

more recently in the Ladakh region—demonstrate the danger that it poses to America's most important strategic partner in South Asia.

Additionally, some U.S. officials, and especially those in the Pentagon, worry that Beijing will seek to establish military bases abroad.[8] In 2019, Beijing inaugurated its first overseas naval base, on the island nation of Djibouti in the Horn of Africa, on the western fringes of the Indian Ocean region—a large, strategic waterway that encompasses littoral states in East Africa and South and Southeast Asia that receive healthy quantums of investment from China.

THE TRUMP ADMINISTRATION'S POLICY RESPONSE: FROM CONCILIATION TO COUNTERBALANCING

Washington views China's five-level foreign policy front as a threat to its interests. But this isn't to suggest the U.S. position toward China has been 100 percent unfriendly in recent years. Early in his presidency, Trump described Xi Jinping as a good friend. Rhetoric toward China was much less harsh. The Belt and Road Initiative rarely came in for criticism.

Only later did Trump's position harden. His administration reacted to the 2020 China-India border spat in Ladakh with unusually sharp and frequent criticism of Beijing; the U.S. government typically says little publicly about India-China border spats. Many senior American leaders—including then-Secretary of State Mike Pompeo—upbraided China for its actions in Ladakh. Meanwhile, Pompeo called Chinese claims in

[8]Benjamin Haas, "China to Set Up Military Bases in Pakistan—Pentagon Report," *The Guardian*, June 7, 2017, https://www.theguardian.com/world/2017/jun/07/china-to-set-up-military-bases-in-pakistan-pentagon-report.

the South China Sea unlawful—the first time Washington had said so publicly about Beijing's claims there. The administration also threatened to impose new travel sanctions on all Chinese Communist Party members. And while the Trump White House would never have been mistaken for a government keen to promote rights and democracy, it excoriated Beijing for its repression of Uighurs.

Several factors account for the downward spiral in the Trump administration's relations with Beijing—factors that go beyond the basic reality of a worsening strategic rivalry. These include a failure to gain traction in negotiations with North Korea. Trump once viewed China as a key mediator between the North Koreans and the Americans. But after a Trump summit with Kim Jong Un failed to move diplomacy forward, China's utility receded. Additionally, the introduction of "wolf warrior diplomacy" did not go down well in Washington. Furthermore, the pandemic and a resultant U.S. economic crisis—both of which unfolded during an election year—gave Trump a strong political incentive to turn hard against China, to blame it for the pandemic, and to accuse it of stealing American jobs.

The essence of the Trump administration's policy toward China was encapsulated in two key policy documents. One was the Trump White House's first national security strategy, released in December 2017, which designated strategic competition as a national security threat. This meant that the administration viewed China, long identified as America's top strategic rival, as a national security threat.[9]

[9]"National Security Strategy of the United States of America," White House, December 2017, https://www.whitehouse.gov/wp-content/uploads/2017/12/NSS-Final-12-18-2017-0905.pdf.

The second key policy document was a White House document, released in May 2020, which outlined its strategic approach to China.[10] It argued that China must be countered—not contained, but countered. The basic argument was that previous U.S. attempts to engage China did not lead Beijing to become a more responsible global stakeholder, and as a result China should be countered. For the Trump administration, this entailed building out its Indo-Pacific strategy, which was meant to operationalize a U.S. vision of a free, open, rules-based Indo Pacific region.

POLICY CONTINUITY FROM THE BIDEN ADMINISTRATION

This general strategy—guided by the imperative of countering China—has remained in place during the early part of the Biden administration. It sent a strong signal from the very start, when it invited Hsiao Bi-khim, Taiwan's de facto ambassador in Washington, to attend Biden's inauguration. This was the first-ever invitation of its kind. Additionally, soon after being confirmed as secretary of state, Antony Blinken affirmed his agreement with Pompeo, his predecessor, that Chinese atrocities against Uighurs constitute genocide. Additionally, the administration's top Asia official, Kurt Campbell, declared that the era of engagement with Beijing has "come to an end," with competition to carry the day.[11] Furthermore, a summit in Alaska

[10]"United States Strategic Approach to the People's Republic of China," White House, May 20, 2020, https://www.whitehouse.gov/wp-content/uploads/2020/05/U.S.-Strategic-Approach-to-The-Peoples-Republic-of-China-Report-5.20.20.pdf.

[11]"Biden's Asia Czar Kurt Campbell Says Era of Engagement with China Is Over," *Bloomberg*, May 26, 2021, https://www.bloomberg.com/news/articles/2021-05-26/biden-s-asia-czar-says-era-of-engagement-with-xi-s-china-is-over.

between senior officials from both countries devolved into a shouting match, and visits to China by senior U.S. officials failed to reduce tensions.

The Biden administration's tough stand shouldn't be surprising. In a January 2020 *Foreign Affairs* essay laying out his foreign policy vision, Biden had written of the need to "get tough with China," and to work with partners to "confront China's abusive behaviors and human rights violations."[12] Wolf warrior diplomacy is problematic for U.S. Republicans and Democrats alike. This is not just because it entails America's top rival throwing its weight around more aggressively on the world stage, but also because—as noted earlier—it poses direct threats to the interests of key U.S. partners like India, treaty allies in East Asia, and friends in Taiwan and Hong Kong—and by extension U.S. interests.

Biden, however, has left open the possibility of cooperation in some spaces. His *Foreign Affairs* article spoke specifically seeking collaboration on climate change, public health, and nonproliferation. The administration's emphasis on working with friends and foes alike to tackle shared global threats suggests a genuine desire to partner with China. However, divergent interests and ill will have carried over from the Trump administration, and such factors will complicate efforts to promote cooperation. In the days before the Biden administration took office, reports surfaced of disagreements within the White House about how much cooperation should

[12]Joseph R. Biden, Jr., "Why America Must Lead Again: U.S. Foreign Policy After Trump," *Foreign Affairs*, January 23, 2020, https://www.foreignaffairs.com/articles/united-states/2020-01-23/why-america-must-lead-again.

be sought.[13] But given the tough tone set during the early months of the administration, the China hawks are likely to have the upper hand.

A rapidly deepening rivalry has given rise to concerns that the world could eventually see a U.S.-China conflict. The scholar Graham Allison has warned of the effect of the "Thucydides Trap"—the idea that given the lessons of history, there's a real possibility that the world's two top powers could one day go to war.[14]

However, there's no reason to believe a U.S.-China conflict is imminent. The Biden administration has showed its commitment to dialogue with Beijing, even though such dialogue hasn't reduced tensions. Longer term prospects for war will depend on how far China goes with its wolf warrior diplomacy. Accordingly, there are two potential triggers that could result in a conflict. One is a Chinese attempt to seize territory or stage attacks in the waters of the Indo Pacific. Territorial disputes there involve key U.S. allies, including the Philippines in the South China Sea dispute and Japan in the Senkaku Islands dispute. Another potential trigger is China's use of force in Taiwan. While current U.S. policy does not require America to come to Taiwan's defense under such a scenario, an increasingly hostile U.S.-China relationship means that one can't rule out the possibility of Washington changing course.[15]

[13]Thomas Wright, "The Risk of John Kerry Following His Own China Policy," *The Atlantic*, December 22, 2020, https://www.theatlantic.com/ideas/archive/2020/12/risk-john-kerry-following-his-own-china-policy/617459/.

[14]Graham Allison, *Destined for War: Can America and China Escape Thucydides's Trap?* (New York: Houghton Mifflin Harcourt, 2017).

[15]See Richard Bush, "The United States Security Partnership with Taiwan," Brookings Institution, November 2016, https://www.brookings.

CONTENDING VIEWS ON U.S.-CHINA RIVALRY

Is countering Beijing the right U.S. policy? The conventional wisdom says yes: Beijing has adapted an increasingly muscular and aggressive policy—one that undercuts U.S. interests and those of its allies and friends—and it's therefore important for America to push back. It's also important to telegraph a message of toughness to a Chinese government that likely implemented its wolf warrior diplomacy in part because of a perception of flagging U.S. global strength.

There are, however, costs to a confrontational U.S. policy. It limits opportunities for cooperation in a world where America and China actually share interests in multiple spaces. These include counterterrorism and infrastructure development. If a U.S. policymaker were to look at the Belt and Road Initiative from a purely economic standpoint—one that views BRI as an effort to create much-needed infrastructure, to reduce poverty, to generate employment, and so on—then she would have no reason to oppose it, given that such intended outcomes are backed by Washington. Only when the policymaker looks at BRI through a strategic lens, and views it as a vehicle for an expansion of China's footprint, and as a potential Trojan horse for Chinese military expansionism—only then does U.S. opposition set in.

The combination of shared interests and poor relations with China results in numerous squandered opportunities for Washington—including an inability to forge deeper

edu/wp-content/uploads/2016/11/fp_20160713_ taiwan_alliance.pdf and John Xie, "Will US Make Clear-cut Commitment to Defend Taiwan from China?" Voice of America, August 21, 2020, https://www.voanews.com/east-asia-pacific/voa-news-china/will-us-make-clear-cut-commitment-defend-taiwan-china.

cooperation on Afghanistan, a place where Washington and Beijing see eye to eye, with their shared support for a more stable, prosperous, and regionally connected Afghanistan.

So, do current circumstances truly warrant a tough policy against China? Does the United States overestimate and exaggerate Chinese aggression? In effect, is wolf warrior diplomacy actually a case of a sheep in wolf's clothing? Kishore Mahbubani, a prominent China dove, certainly believes so:

> Since China is not mounting a military force to threaten or invade the United States, not trying to intervene in America's domestic politics, and not engaged in a deliberate campaign to destroy the American economy, we must consider that, in spite of the increasing clamor about the threat China poses to the United States, it is still possible for America to find a way to deal peaceably with a China that will become the number one economic, and possibly geopolitical, power within a decade.[16]

Mahbubani's view is that America should accept China's rise and accept it as a major power, while also strengthening international rules and partnerships to keep China's influence in check. This entails throwing its full support behind organizations like the WTO that can rein in improper Chinese trade policies, and UN legal conventions that can constrain Beijing's assertiveness in the South China Sea.

Such a position holds relevance for the Biden administration, and dovetails with its desire to work multilaterally, through international institutions, to achieve common goals with like-minded states. One of the administration's objectives is to build a

[16]Kishore Mahbubani, "What China Threat? How the United States and China Can Avoid War," *Harper's Magazine*, February 2019, https://harpers.org/archive/2019/02/what-china-threat/.

broader global consensus in favor of developing alternative mechanisms and initiatives that drive countries—especially those in Asia—away from Chinese investment and influence, and more toward U.S.-sponsored alternatives. A new project announced by the G-7 in 2021 to develop an alternative global infrastructure corridor is illustrative. However, given the size and scope of Beijing's BRI, developing a better alternative amounts to a very tall order.

MANAGING CHINA'S RISE

Any U.S. response, however, will be anchored to the Indo-Pacific strategy, the Trump administration's core Asia policy and one the Biden administration appears keen to retain.[17] The strategy is meant to counterbalance China through the establishment and promotion of a free and open rules-based system. If successful, it can build a consensus around principles and norms that constrain China's influence.

The India-China border spat in Ladakh crystallizes the importance of the Indo-Pacific strategy and the rationale behind it. The crisis marked a clear provocation by Beijing. It represented an attempt to bully a smaller neighbor with the use of force, and a threat to the free and open and rights- and rules-based vision—those key catchphrases from the Indo-Pacific strategy—that Washington believes can help bring about peace and prosperity.

On some levels, the Indo-Pacific policy resembles the Asia pivot and rebalance policies of the Obama era. Those initiatives

[17]For a detailed articulation of this policy, see "A Free and Open Indo Pacific: Advancing a Shared Vision," U.S. Department of State, November 4, 2019, https://www.state.gov/wp-content/uploads/2019/11/Free-and-Open-Indo-Pacific-4Nov2019.pdf.

had limited success, as Washington struggled to convince skeptical Asian capitals and publics that America was seriously committed to reallocating resources to Asia. What's different about the Indo-Pacific strategy is that it includes additional facilitative mechanisms that put more meat on the policy's bones. The BUILD Act, signed by Trump in 2018, hastens America's ability to deploy resources for overseas investments through the formation of a new U.S. development agency—the International Development Finance Corporation. There is also the Blue Dot Network, a due diligence tool meant to certify potential infrastructure projects as transparent and sustainable, so that investors are comfortable deploying capital to these projects.[18]

The contrast with China's infrastructure investments—which Washington depicts as featuring opaque contracts, inequitable exploitation of local resources, and debt-generating loans—is unmistakable. Taken together, these new financial tools can compliment the security-focused hardware—a revitalized Quadrilateral Security Dialogue, deepening maritime cooperation, a scaled-up military partnership with India—associated with the Indo-Pacific strategy.

Several factors will determine the effectiveness of these new tools, and how much they help America counterbalance Chinese power in Asia.

[18]There are opportunities for Washington, in some parts of the region, to cooperate with India on new infrastructure investments. In recent years, New Delhi has concluded energy deals with Bangladesh, Myanmar, Nepal, and Sri Lanka. These new initiatives, perhaps under the aegis of BIMSTEC, can become collaborative ventures with the United States. See Michael Kugelman, "Opinion: To Push Back China's Belt and Road Initiative Will Be India's Main Challenge," *Outlook India*, July 6, 2020, https://magazine.outlookindia.com/story/india-news-opinion-to-push-back-chinas-growing-belt-and-road-initiative-will-be-indias-main-challenge/303385.

The first relates to interests. Will the volatilities of Mideast geopolitics constrain U.S. efforts to redirect bandwidth and resources to the Indo- Pacific? It is common in Washington to hear that this is the Asian century, and that America is a Pacific power. However, many vital U.S. foreign policy interests are still anchored to the Middle East—home to many top American allies and rivals, and to conflicts that include or impact the United States. A conflict in 2021 between Israel, one of America's closest allies, and Gaza served as one more sobering reminder of just how closely U.S. interests and concerns remain intertwined with the region. Indeed, while the U.S. shale gas revolution, and America's lessening dependence on Middle East oil, may untether Washington a bit from the region, its interests remain strong there—and this is a view with strong bipartisan support.

The second relates to diplomacy. Can America enlist a critical mass of partners in its efforts to push back against China? The Quad and G-7 countries appear to be onboard, but what beyond that? Beijing's wolf warrior diplomacy is sharpening global sentiment against China. But the world's buy-in for a U.S.-led push against Beijing shouldn't be taken for granted. Countries in Southeast Asia that value Chinese economic support—even while continuing to depend on the American security umbrella—may not wish to risk antagonizing Beijing. Similarly, the smaller countries of South Asia—Bangladesh, the Maldives, Nepal, and Sri Lanka—demonstrate an interest in retaining cordial relations with both Beijing and New Delhi. The world isn't neatly falling into two different camps—one pro-China, one pro-America. It's a reality that undercuts the argument, advanced by some analysts, that we are witnessing the emergence of a new Cold War.[19]

The third relates to preferences. Will nations be willing to support new U.S.-led infrastructure initiatives that take longer to materialize, require more scrutiny, and carry more conditionalities (such as assurances of transparency and sustainability) than those overseen by China under the BRI rubric?

CONCLUSION

U.S.-China rivalry is here to say. How Washington manages its troubled relationship with Beijing holds major implications for a world order that is in considerable flux. It could trigger a resurgence in multilateralism that helps bring some balance and stability to a world dominated by a dangerous great-power rivalry. Or it could usher in an increasingly hostile confrontation. Either way, China will remain America's top foreign policy priority for years to come.

(Michael Kugelman is Asia Program deputy director and senior associate for South Asia at the Woodrow Wilson International Center for Scholars in Washington, DC).

[19]Quite a few analysts, in fact, have pushed back against the idea of a new U.S.-China cold war. See, for example, Thomas Christensen, "There Will Not Be a New Cold War," *Foreign Affairs*, March 24, 2021, https://www.foreignaffairs.com/articles/united-states/2021-03-24/there-will-not-be-new-cold-war.

Chapter 11

Chinese Inroads into Latin America: Why, What and How?

– Dr Shaheli Das

Historically there has been limited interest of politicians and academicians in the subject of Sino-Latin American relations. This has altered as a result of the People's Republic of China's (PRC) striking economic development trajectory post the initiation of economic reform policies of greater openness towards the global economy since the 1970s. Over the years, with a surge in industrialisation and internationalisation, Beijing's economic interest in the developing nations has risen. In the same period, China became increasingly important for the countries in the Latin American region.[1] In this context this work discusses Chinese inroads into the Latin American region, the Asian giant's real motive there and most importantly the Latin American response. The central argument of this work is that China's foreign policy in the region is largely commercially driven over and above its strategic objectives.

[1]Cui, Shoujun and Manuel Pérez García (2016), "China and Latin America in Transition: Policy Dynamics, Economic Commitments, and Social Impacts", [Online: Web] Accessed on 11 December 2018, URL: https://link.springer.com/book/10.1057%2F978-1-137-54080-5#about

Interestingly, in comparison to China's association with the other regions of the world, the country's engagement with Latin America is dynamic. The PRC now seeks to look beyond its East Asian neighbours and forge ties with countries in the distant frontiers that could boost its reputation in the international sphere. In this context, countries in Latin America are important to it. The nations in these three regions fit well within the framework of China's desire to associate itself with greater number of developing nations across the globe. Their engagement form a model of South-South cooperation.

THE RATIONALE BEHIND CHINA'S ENGAGEMENT WITH LATIN AMERICA

China's interest in the region can be broadly grouped into two distinct categories: maximalist objectives and the minimalist objectives. The maximalist goal refers to China's desire to attain a great power status. There are two aspects to this goal: economic and political. Interestingly, Latin America is valuable to fulfil this objective from both the angles. Economically, in order to sustain its domestic economic boom and as a resource-intensive nation, China seeks to attain raw materials from the LACs and diversify the source of such imports.[2] The region is also viewed by the Chinese as a stable market for the export of its manufactured goods. Consequently, Chinese investors have ventured into the region to obtain stakes in the natural resource firms, offer credits to petroleum as well as mining investors, and prepar-

[2]Das, Shaheli (2016), "How Important Is Latin America on China's Foreign Policy Agenda?", [Online: Web] Accessed on 11 December 2018, URL: https://thediplomat.com/2016/11/how-important-is-latin-america-on-chinas-foreignpolicy-agenda/

ing long-term acquisition contracts for mineral and oil in the region.[3]

Politically, in order to attain its twin centenary goals of instituting a moderately prosperous society by 2020[4] as well as developing a moderately socialist nation by the middle of the 21st century, China seeks to adhere to an independent foreign policy. Consequently, China desires to construct a new type of international relations.[5] At the core of this strategy is the idea of forging constructive ties with the other developing nations across the world. Also given the ongoing Sino-US power transition, China seeks to construct a multipolar world that would comprise of restructuring the global order, reforming the international financial institutions as well as bodies of global governance such as the World Bank, International Monetary Fund (IMF) and the United Nations (UN) (Stuenkel 2010a). To this end, the Belt and Road Initiative (BRI), construction of multilateral development banks such as the New Development Bank (NDB) and Asian Infrastructure Investment Bank (AIIB) may be recognized as chief contributions to global governance reform. As founding member of these key projects and institutions, China seeks to

[3]Kotschwar, Barbara and Theodore Moran and Julia Muir (2012), "Chinese Investment in Latin American Resources: The Good, the Bad, and the Ugly", [Online: Web] Accessed on 11 December 2018, URL: https://www.researchgate.net/publication/254423827_Chinese_Investment_in_Latin_American_Resources_The_Good_the_Bad_and_the_Ugly

[4]Fornes, Gaston and Alvaro Mendez (2018), "The China-Latin America Axis", [Online: Web] Accessed on 11 December 2018, URL: https://link.springer.com/book/10.1007%2F978-3-319-66721-8#about

[5]Aberg, John Hugo Simon (2017), "Status, revisionism, and great power strategy : US China positional competition and the struggle for leadership in Asia-Pacific", [Online: Web] Accessed on 11 December 2018, URL: https://commons. ln.edu.hk/cgi/viewcontent.cgi?referer=&httpsredir=1&=&article=1019&context=pol_etd

surge its influence in shaping the norms of global governance and consequently accomplish its objective of becoming a principal player in the international arena. Latin America comprises of 33 nations, of which China maintains diplomatic ties with as many as 24 countries – a number that is big enough for Beijing to identify this region with great importance in its foreign policy agenda. Therefore, China seeks active engagement and participation of the Latin American countries (LACs) in its landmark projects and initiatives. Effective support from the LACs in its pilot projects and initiatives would definitely offer a boost to China, allowing it to move a step further towards attaining a great power status.

The minimalist objective refers to displacing the Republic of China (ROC), popularly known as Taiwan in Latin America through the announcement of the One-China policy as the basis of its diplomatic ties with the LACs. Essentially, the PRC has used economic diplomacy to lure the LACs towards it through arrangements such as foreign direct investment (FDI), loans and funding large-scale infrastructure projects in the region. Given the fact that China has emerged as the largest creditor of the nations in the region that have instituted diplomatic ties with the PRC (Rand Corporation 2018), the remaining nations in the region have started viewing their engagement with China as a beneficial prospect. A case in point is the recent trend of the LACs namely Dominican Republic (2017), Panama (2017) and El Salvador (2018) switching diplomatic ties with the PRC.

Having discussed the brief points of the PRC's intent in the Latin American region, the following section would discuss China's two fold interests in the region in detail:

I. Strategic Interests

II. Economic Interests

I. CHINA'S STRATEGIC INTERESTS IN THE REGION

China has entered a decisive phase in terms of attaining the nation's rejuvenation. With regard to its objective of attaining the twin centenary goals, Beijing has been advancing the growth and evolution of a socialist democracy, socialist market economy,[6] and an ecological civilization with a harmonious society. In this context, China seeks to pursue an independent foreign policy and put into practice its opening up policy.[7] Therefore, the country adheres to the strategy of developing a 'new type of international relations'.[8] This principally signifies to the development of constructive ties with other emerging powers across the globe, which comprises of the LACs.

The MFA, PRC has continuously reiterated that peaceful co-existence, inclusiveness, openness as well as seeking common development are key objectives of the country's foreign policy. The PRC also maintains that despite its economic growth over the decades, its national condition of being a developing nation remains unchanged. Further, to ensure its peaceful development, China seeks a peaceful international environment. As a developing nation itself, the country seeks to strengthen solidarity with other developing nations such as the LACs. In this context, Premier Wen Jiabao mentioned in his address at the UNECLAC

[6]MFA,PRC (2016a), "China's Policy Paper on Latin America and the Caribbean", November 24, 2016, [Online: Web] Accessed 8 October 2018, URL: http://www.fmprc.gov.cn/mfa_eng/zxxx_662805/t1418254.shtml

[7]Soto, Juan Alfredo (2009), "Diplomatic Competition Between China and Taiwan in Latin America", [Online: Web] Accessed on 12 August 2019, URL: http://etd.lib.nsysu.edu.tw/ETD-db/ETD-search/getfile?URN=etd-0811109-110914&filename=etd-0811109-110914.pdf

[8]MFA,PRC (2016a), "China's Policy Paper on Latin America and the Caribbean", November 24, 2016, [Online: Web] Accessed 8 October 2018, URL: http://www.fmprc.gov.cn/mfa_eng/zxxx_662805/t1418254.shtml

that to forge deeper ties with the LACs, China seeks to pursue the mechanisms of increasing high level contacts, instituting various government consultation mechanisms, increasing exchanges between political parties, legislatures and local governments, augmenting experience sharing on governance related issues, promoting common interests with a special focus on trade and economic cooperation and maintenance of food security through agricultural cooperation.[9] Infact the PRC's ties with Latin America are symbolic of the paradigm of South-South cooperation. In this context, Hua Chunying, Chinese Foreign Ministry spokesperson has said, "China, and Latin American and Caribbean countries are all developing. To expand cooperation is in their common interest, and is also an important component of South-South cooperation".

A reason for the swift development of thriving ties between China and the LACs is the fact that China takes the case of each LAC on its own terms. A case in point is Cuba. While engaging with Cuba, the PRC very often hails their common revolutionary history.[10] However, in the case of its association with some other countries such as Venezuela and Argentina, which possess faltering economies, it is finance that dominates the discussions and engagements. Nonetheless, the developing nation card always forms the base of China's association with all LACs.

[9]MFA,PRC (2012), "Address by Premier Wen Jiabao at the Economic Commission for Latin America and the Caribbean of the United Nations", [Online: Web] Accessed 14 September 2018, URL: http://www.fmprc.gov.cn/mfa_eng/topics_665678/wjbcxlhgkcxfzdhbfwbxwlgzlagt_665712/t945728.shtml

[10]XinhuaNet (2018d), "Xi holds talks with Cuban president to advance ties", [Online: Web] Accessed on 11 August 2019, URL: http://www.xinhuanet.com/english/2018-11/08/c_137592812.htm

While discussing about South- South cooperation and China's engagement with the LACs, mention must be made of the China-CELAC Forum. Indeed this forum is symbolic of the comprehensive cooperation between the two sides. In this regard, Yin Hengmin, special representative of the PRC on Latin American affairs said, "The China-CELAC forum has yielded delightful early results, which has laid a solid basis for the long-term development of the all-round cooperation between China and Latin America".

In 2008 the first policy paper on the region was published by the government of the PRC wherein the objective of instituting a "cooperative and comprehensive partnership" with Latin America was emphasized, based on the tenets of common development, mutual benefit and equality with the LACs.[11] Importantly, the document reiterated that China identifies its ties with the LACs from a strategic angle, and One-China principle would remain the political basis for the institution and advancement of relations between the two parties. The White Paper mentions,

> "The overwhelming majority of countries in the region are committed to the One-China policy and the position of supporting China's reunification and not having official ties or contacts with Taiwan. The Chinese Government appreciates such a stance. China is ready to establish and develop state-to-state relations with all Latin American and Caribbean countries based on the One-China principle".[12]

[11]Fornes, Gaston and Alvaro Mendez (2018), "The China-Latin America Axis", [Online: Web] Accessed on 11 December 2018, URL: https://link.springer.com/book/10.1007%2F978-3-319-66721-8#about

[12]MFA,PRC (2008), "China's Policy Paper on Latin America and the Caribbean", [Online: Web] Accessed on 3 October 2018, URL: http://www.gov.cn/english/official/2008-11/05/content_1140347.htm

Key to Chinese interests in forging closer ties with the LACs is the idea that reinforcing solidarity with other developing nations has been a cornerstone of China's foreign policy.

Two factors have greatly contributed to such relations: first, China shares an identical history with most developing nations, therefore they understand each other and possess similar desires and demands. Second, Beijing adheres to the principle of merging patriotism with Marxist internationalism in its foreign policy. Thus, China ascertains its position on international affairs based on the merit of each case as well as in accordance to the underlying interest of people of China and the world as a whole.[13] Essentially China's interest in developing ties with Latin America must be viewed from this perspective.

Further, China is gradually moving away from the idea of 'Third World-ism' towards the promotion of the idea of multilateralism. To attain this objective, the PRC requires a network of allies from the Third World, including the countries of Latin America. After a decisive victory in what could have been the first official censure by the UN Human Rights Council in 1995, Beijing has progressively sought the votes of the Latin American nations at the UN as well as at other international forums to counterbalance the US influence. Latin America also appears in Beijing's larger framework of advocating its version of "democracy in international relations" (*guoji guanxi minzhuhua*) i.e. creating a multipolar economic and political international order wherein the Middle Kingdom (*Zhongguo*) revives its customary position at the core of international affairs.[14]

[13]Yang, Fuchang(2002), "China's Relations with Developing countries", in Yang Fuchang (eds.) *Contemporary China and its Foreign Policy,* Beijing: World Affairs Press

[14]Pham, Peter.J. (2010), "China's Strategic Penetration of Latin America: What it Means for US Interests", *American Foreign Policy Interests*, 32(6): 363-381.

Thus, these are the chief strategic interests of the PRC in the region. In the following section, a detailed discussion of the country's commercial drivers into the LACs has been made.

II. China's Economic Interests in the Region

The principal argument of this work is that in the 21st century China is driven into the continent primarily by its economic objectives over and above its strategic interests. Thus, a brief discussion has been made on China's economic status as it stands at this point of time.

China's Economic Status

The first important issue of deliberation is China's developing country status. In this context it may be said that, economic development remains the prime objective of the country, while the country's foreign policy seeks to foster a stable, peaceful and cooperative external environment that would champion China's internal development efforts. There are various perspectives to China's developing country status. One view suggests that the world is not convinced about Beijing being a developing nation, given its rising strength in economy, defence, science and technology and soft power. Another view holds that although China has undergone a huge transformation in the last 30 years, the country lags in several areas.

China is at present deeply engaged with the current international economic and financial system. After a five-year delay of approval by the US Congress, the country's voting rights in the International Monetary Fund (IMF) have finally risen from 3.8 percent[15] to 6.09 percent.[16] Further in early 2016, China became a full member of the European Bank for Reconstruction and Development. The country has also taken the initiative to establish and is the principal founding member of the AIIB.[17]

There seem to be a number of reasons owing to which economic development is of prime importance to China. First, the PRC's foreign policy towards the region is conditioned by the country's internal priorities such as economic growth, political stability and regional security. The Chinese government seeks to maintain internal political stability, through the instruments of continued economic growth and nationalism. Internally, these factors have also served as a source of legitimacy for the CCP due to two reasons: first, it has raised the standard of living of the people of China and has been a source of national pride in turn contributing to nationalism. Externally, such growth is a foundation for the emergence of the PRC as an international great power. Thus, to sustain the present level of economic growth the country becomes increasingly reliant on foreign resources from regions like Africa, Central Asia and Latin America. In this context, the factors driving China into Latin America is directly related to the country's foreign policy priorities.

[15]BBC (2015),"IMF Reforms Clear Last Hurdle With US Adoption", [Online: Web] Accessed on 3 June 2018, URL: https://www.bbc.com/news/business-35141683

[16]International Monetary Fund (2018), "IMF Members' Quotas and Voting Power, and IMF Board of Governors", [Online: Web] Accessed 6 October, 2018, URL: https://www.imf.org/external/np/sec/memdir/members.aspx

[17]MFA,PRC (2016c), "The Belt and Road: China's Initiative, Contribution to the World", [Online: Web] Accessed on 13 February, 2017, URL: http://www.fmprc.gov.cn/mfa_eng/wjb_663304/zwjg_665342/zwbd_665378/t 136090 2.shtml

Second, out of a population of 1.3 billion in China, as many as 700 million or over half reside in rural areas – a number that is higher than in developed nations. Further, 150 million people in the country continue to live on under a dollar a day, the poverty line determined by the UN.

Third, significant disparities exist between urban and rural areas as well as between the various regions in the country. The per capita GDP of eastern China is atleast three times higher than that of western China.

Fourth, China's investment in R&D accounted for 2.1 percent of the GDP in 2016, just crossing the 2 percent threshold expected for nations with a reasonable innovative capacity.[18]

It is also important to mention here that there is definitely some level of economic reciprocity as the basis of development of Sino-Latin American economic relations. There are two interrelated aspects to this issue of mutual benefits. First, to sustain its social and economic development in sustainable ways, there has been a trend of rising demand in China's domestic market for food, metals, energy and minerals. Such rise in domestic demand in China has definitely benefitted the export-oriented nations in Latin America. This, in turn, has boosted the social and economic development of these countries.

Second, the country has a population of more than 1.3 billion people and offers a huge market as well as is a source of great opportunities for the LAC in terms of trade and investment.[19]

[18]MFA,PRC (2010), "Peace, Development and Cooperation: Themes of China's Foreign Policy", [Online: Web] Accessed 7 October 2018, URL: https://www.fmprc.gov.cn/mfa_eng/topics_665678/cpop_665770/t708041.shtml

[19]Liu, Yongtao (2012), "Promote China-Latin American Relations in the 21st Century", Globalization, *Competitiveness and Governability Journal*, 6(1)107-114, URL: https://gcg.universia.net/article/viewFile/422/548

In this regard, economist Zhao Changhui, from the China Society for International Finance stated, "China needs the region's commodities and resources" and "at the same time, countries in the region are looking for ways to move away from the traditional geopolitics in which the United States plays a heavily dominant role".[20]

Thus, there exists significant degree of reciprocity in the relationship between the two sides. When viewed from this perspective it seems evident that the China's prime drivers in the region is the fulfilment of its economic objectives over and above the country's strategic interests.

China's Economic Objectives in the Region

In the recent years despite the international financial crisis and its aftermath, the robust economic growth of China has pushed the "Middle Kingdom" to explore beyond its traditional commercial and trading partners, and take a fresh look at regions such as Latin America, both for new markets as well as for supplies of resources/ raw materials. The country's rising demand for natural resources, namely iron ore, oil, copper, aluminium, and abundant foreign reserves has pushed Beijing to obtain few of these strategic resources in such a way that the global media houses have addressed it as a 'shopping spree' of China.[21] Such a strategy is coherent with the PRC's[22] association with other developing nations as with the LACs.

[20]South China Morning Post (2015), "China president vows to double annual trade with Latin America to 500bn dollars", BBC Monitoring Global News IDSA, Hong Kong, 9 January 2015.

[21]Barragán, Juan Manuel Gil and Castillo, Andrés Aguilera (2016), "China and Latin America: strategic partners or competitors?", [Online: Web] Accessed on 12 August 2019, URL: http://www.redalyc.org/pdf/206/20652069001.pdf

[22]Wenhua, Shan and Kimmo, Nuotio and Kangle, Zhang (2018), *Normative Readings of the Belt and Road Initiative*, Cham: Springer, [Online: Web] Accessed on 12 August 2019, URL: https://link.springer.com/book/10.1007%2F978-3-319-78018-4#toc

With the growth in its financial influence, the PRC now ventures out to accomplish certain objectives: (a) to obtain recognition of full market status, (b) to secure the resources the country necessitates and expand the source of such imports so as to curtail the PRC's vulnerability, and (c) to preserve the country's access to foreign markets in order to safeguard the export of its finished goods.[23] Owing to the above-mentioned factors, Latin America weighs high on China's foreign policy agenda.[24]

Interestingly, internationalisation of the yuan is another objective of China in the region. The PRC is promoting its currency in its trade with the region, especially with regard to its payments for food and minerals. The ostensible objective of the country has been to reinforce its usage as a reserve currency as well as to facilitate the procurement of China's capital commodities and trade.[25]

In 2000, during the administration of President Jiang Zemin and Premier Zhu Rongji, the country commenced the going out (*zouchuqu zhanlue*) policy so as to ascertain a steady transfer of resources, chief to preserve the PRC's meteoric economic growth.[26] Around this time, the MOFCOM, PRC stated that as for the country's going-out policy with regard to energy security,[27]

[23]He, Li (2007), "China's Growing Interest in Latin America and its Implications", *Journal of Strategic Studies*, 30(4-5): 833-862

[24]Das, Shaheli (2017), "China's Rising Footprint into Latin America: Geopolitics, Economics or Both?", [Online: Web] Accessed on 11 August 2019, URL: http://utsynergyjournal.org/2017/02/10/chinas-rising-footprint-into-latin-americageopolitics-economics-or-both/

[25]Stabroek News (2012), "Guyanese paper says Caribbean region must enhance ties with China", BBC Monitoring Global News IDSA, Georgetown, 12 August 2012.

[26]Das, Shaheli (2017a), "China's Rising Footprint into Latin America: Geopolitics, Economics or Both?", [Online: Web] Accessed on 11 August 2019, URL: http://utsynergyjournal.org/2017/02/10/chinas-rising-footprint-into-latin-americageopolitics-economics-or-both/

[27]*Ibid*

it had recognised Latin America as one of the three chief areas – together with Middle East/Africa and Russia/Central Asia[28] – which could likely evolve as net energy suppliers for Beijing in the forthcoming years.[29]

Thus, these are some of China's key economic drivers to the region. The following section discusses the economic ties between the two sides in some detail.

SINO-LATIN AMERICAN COMMERCIAL RELATIONS

Commercial ties between China and Latin America have shot up, especially in the last two decades. This has happened through two principal mechanisms, first being trade and second being capital inflows in the shape of lending and FDI.[30] In the following sections these mechanisms have been discussed in detail.

China's Trade with Latin America

The PRC's bilateral trade with the LACs have elevated from the US$241.5 billion[31] mark in 2000 and touched US$260 billion in

[28] He, Li (2007), "China's Growing Interest in Latin America and its Implications", *Journal of Strategic Studies*, 30(4-5): 833-862

[29] Jenkins, Rhys (2012), "Latin America and China – A New Dependency?", *Third World Quarterly*, 33(7): 1337-1358.

[30] Gonzalez, Anabel (2018), "Latin America-China Trade and Investment Amid Global Tensions: A Need To Upgrade and Diversify", [Online: Web] Accessed on 22 May 2019, URL:https://www.atlanticcouncil.org/images/publications/Latin-America-China-Trade-and-Investment-Amid-Global-Tensions.pdf

[31] MFA,PRC (2012), "Address by Premier Wen Jiabao at the Economic Commission for Latin America and the Caribbean of the United Nations", [Online: Web] Accessed 14 September 2018, URL: http://www.fmprc.gov.cn/mfa_eng/topics_665678/wjbcxlhgkcxfzdhbfwbxwlgzlagt_665712/t945728.shtml

2017.[32] The figure below depicts trade flow between the PRC and the LACs in the period from 2001 to 2015.[33]

Figure 1: Bilateral Trade China-LACs 2001-2015

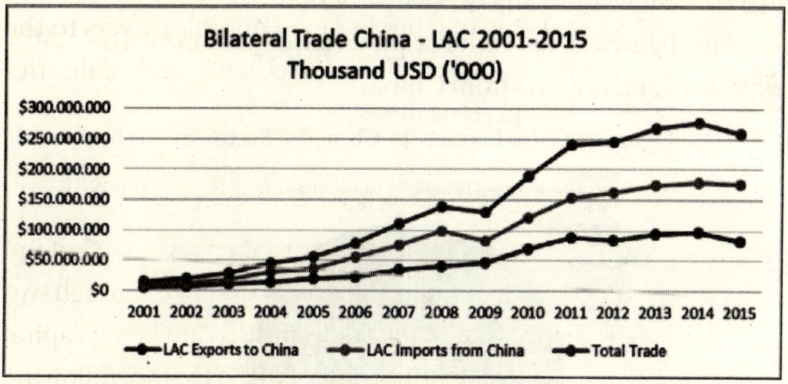

Source: Juan Manuel Gil Barragan and Andres Aguilera Castillo, 2017.

At present, China ranks as Latin America's second largest trading partner after United States. Infact in the last 15 years, Latin American growth has been largely driven by Beijing's procurement of commodities. According to MOFCOM, as of 2017, the volume of import of China from Latin America reached USD 127.02 billion, up by 23.68 percent from the 2016 mark.[34] While commenting on the state of Sino-Latin American commercial ties President Xi said,

[32]Das, Shaheli (2019), "With China slowing down, India's burgeoning role in Latin America assumes significance", [Online: Web] Accessed on 11 August 2019, URL: https://www.financialexpress.com/defence/with-china-slowing-down-indiasburgeoning-role-in-latin-america-asssumes-significance/1475854/

[33]Rosales, Osvaldo (2013), "For a Quality Leap in Business Relations Between China and Latin America and the Caribbean", [Online: Web] Accessed on 12 August 2019, URL: https://cadmus.eui.eu/bitstream/handle/1814/27704/RSCAS_PP_%202013_12.pdf?sequence=1

[34]Xinhua(2018a), "China becomes second largest trading partner of Latin America", [Online: Web] Accessed on 11 December 2018, URL: http://www.xinhuanet.com/english/2018-11/29/c_137640261.htm

"Today, China has become the second largest trading partner of Latin America and the Caribbean, and Latin America and the Caribbean a major destination for outbound Chinese investment, second only to Asia".[35]

The figures below offer a pictorial depiction of the LACs' exports to and imports from China.

Figure 2: LACs Exports to China by Sector in 2016

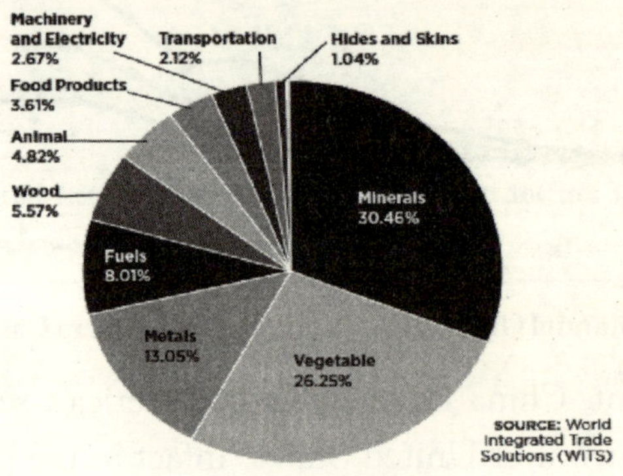

Source: Gonzalez 2018

Figure 3: LACs Imports From China by Sector in 2016

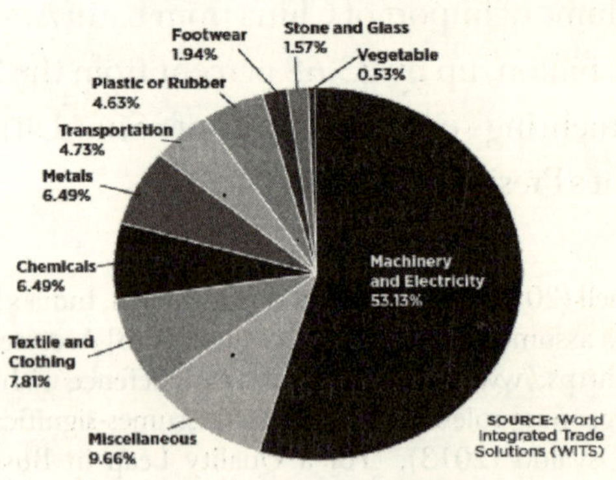

Source: Gonzalez 2018

[35] People's Daily (2016), "Quotable quotes from President Xi's speech at Peruvian Congress", [Online: Web] Accessed on 11 August 2019, URL: http://en.people.cn/n3/2016/1122/c90000-9145336.html

Chinese Investment in Latin America

Although the region is geographically remote, Latin America is well-endowed with natural resources. By making investments in Latin America, Beijing seeks to gain easier access to these resources. Besides, the region comprises of a large market with a total GDP of USD 5.7 trillion and as many as 600 million consumers that have close proximity to the US market. Therefore, it interests China to readily enter the world's largest market through the so-called "spring board effect".

Various Chinese companies have also made inroads into Latin America. For example, Huawei, a Chinese multinational networking, telecommunications equipment and services company, had entered the markets of the LACs in 1998 and at present operates in Mexico, Brazil, Venezuela, Colombia, and other key nations in the region.

In 2010, Lenovo engaged itself in investment in modern agriculture in the region, and in August 2012, the company established Joyvio Group. As of now, the group has obtained a joint stock farm and four fully owned farms in Chile. The objective of Joyvio is to become Chile's largest fresh fruit exporter to Beijing.[36]

Chinese venture capital investment in the region has soared to $1 billion since early 2017, compared to about $30 million in 2015. Chinese start-ups that have been making an endeavour to make inroads into the region include Hangzhou based Tian Ge Interactive Holdings Ltd, which seeks to develop an internet finance platform in Mexico. Phonemaker Transsion Holdings has also been making arrangements to set up operations in Colombia.

[36] People's Daily (2014), "Chinese Companies in Latin America: Transforming From Speed To Quality", [Online: Web] Accessed 14 July 2018, URL: http://en.people.cn/98649/8622712.html

Similarly, China Mobile Games and Entertainment Group seeks to distribute mobile games in Mexico.[37]

The region seems to be an ideal place for Chinese investment in energy. The acquisition of the Pacific Hydro Brazil by the State Power Investment Corp (SPIC) is an example to this end.

Interestingly China has been granting credit or loans to the LACs in diverse forms and for different purposes. Such is the case, for instance of Venezuela. From 2008 to 2015, the China Development Bank offered loans worth US$37 billion to Venezuela. However, the disbursement of the loan was within the framework of oil-for-loan arrangement. This necessitated the state oil enterprise PDVSA to dispatch barrels of oil to China every year. Venezuela caters between four and five percent of Beijing's oil imports. However, in October 2014, as an expression of goodwill the CDB had decided to do away with the minimum daily deliveries, so that this LAC could vend out more number of barrels for cash to other nations.[38]

Loans have also been offered by China to the various LACs to facilitate infrastructure construction as well as to advance their overall socio-economic development. For instance, in 2015 Costa Rica received a loan worth $395 million from Beijing to expand Route 32, which comprised of 105 kilometres and traversed from Caribbean town of Puerto Limon to Pococi. However, the loan entailed the obligation to the Costa Rican government to appoint a Chinese construction firm named China Harbour Engineering

[37]Riley, Michael and Jorden Robertson (2018), "New Evidence of Hacked Supermicro Hardware found in US Telecom", [Online: Web] Accessed 13 October 2018, URL: https://www.bloomberg.com/news/articles/2018-10-09/new-evidence-of-hackedsupermicro-hardware-found-in-u-s-telecom

[38]El Nacional (2015), "Chinese state bank in predicament with loans-for-oil scheme with Venezuela", BBC Monitoring Global News IDSA, Caracas, 19 June 2015.

Company (CHEC) to assist the country in expanding the artery highway.[39]

The table below offers an overview of the nature of investments made by the various Chinese firms in the various LACs between 2005 and 2019.

Table 1: Investment by Chinese Firms in the Various LACs Between 2005 and 2019

China Global Investment Tracker

Dataset 1 Investments

Year	Month	Investor	Quantity in Millions	Share Size	Transaction Pa	Sector	Subsector	Country	Region	BRI	Gre
2005	January	Minmetals	$500		Cubapetroleo	Metals		Cuba	North America		G
2005	February	Minmetals	$550	50%	Codelco	Metals	Copper	Chile	South America		G
2005	September	CNPC, Sinopec	$1,420		EnCana	Energy	Oil	Ecuador	South America		
2006	September	Sinopec	$430	50%	Omimex	Energy	Oil	Colombia	South America		
2007	February	Zijin Mining, China Nonferrous, Xiamen C&D	$190	45%, 35%, 2	Monterrico	Metals	Copper	Peru	South America		
2007	June	Chinalco	$790	100%	Peru Copper	Metals	Copper	Peru	South America		
2007	July	Golden Dragon	$100	100%		Metals	Copper	Mexico	North America		G
2007	December	Minmetals, Jiangxi Copper	$450	100%	Northern Peru (	Metals	Copper	Peru	South America		
2008	January	Jinchuan Group	$210		Tyler Resources	Metals		Mexico	North America		
2008	May	Chinalco	$2,180	100%		Metals	Copper	Peru	South America		G
2009	February	Shougang	$990			Metals	Steel	Peru	South America		
2009	May	CNOOC, Sinopec	$320	100%	Talisman Energ	Energy	Oil	Trinidad-Tob	North America		
2009	May	Najinchao	$100	100%	Cardero	Metals	Steel	Peru	South America		
2009	September	State Construction Engineering	$100	3%	Baha Mar Reso	Tourism		Bahamas	North America		G
2009	November	Wuhan Iron and Steel	$400	22%	MMX Mineraca	Metals	Steel	Brazil	South America		
2009	December	CIC	$500		CVRD (Vale)	Metals	Steel	Brazil	South America		
2010	January	China Railway Construction and China Nonferrous	$650	100%	Corriente Reso	Metals	Copper	Ecuador	South America		
2010	January	Shunde Rixin and Minmetals	$1,910	70%		Metals	Steel	Chile	South America		G
2010	February	Sany Heavy	$200	100%		Real estate	Constructic	Brazil	South America		G
2010	March	CNOOC	$3,100	50%	Bridas	Energy		Argentina	South America		
2010	March	East China Mineral Exploration and Development Bureau (Jianç	$1,200		Bernardo de M	Metals	Steel	Brazil	South America		
2010	April	CNPC	$900		PDVSA	Energy	Oil	Venezuela	South America		G
2010	May	Sinochem	$3,070	40%	Statoil	Energy	Oil	Brazil	South America		
2010	May	State Grid	$1,720	100%	Plena Transmis	Energy		Brazil	South America		
2010	June	Shaanxi Chemical	$1,010			Chemicals		Argentina	South America		G
2010	July	Sinomach	$140			Agriculture		Jamaica	North America		
2010	August	Chery Auto	$400			Transport	Autos	Brazil	South America		G
2010	October	Sinopec	$7,100	40%	Repsol	Energy	Oil	Brazil	South America		
2010	October	Minmetals	$2,500	100%		Metals	Copper	Peru	South America		G
2010	November	CNPC, Sinopec	$610			Energy	Oil	Ecuador	South America		G
2010	December	Sinopec	$2,470		Occidental Petr	Energy		Argentina	South America		
2010	December	CIC	$200		BTG Pactual	Finance	Investment	Brazil	South America		
2011	February	CNOOC	$330		ExxonMobil	Energy	Oil	Argentina	South America		
2011	March	Chongqing Grain	$570			Agriculture		Brazil	South America		G
2011	April	ICBC	$100	100%		Finance	Banking	Brazil	South America		G
2011	April	ZTE	$200	100%		Technology	Telecom	Brazil	South America		G
2011	May	Chery Auto	$200	100%		Transport	Autos	Venezuela	South America		G
2011	June	Heilongjiang Beidahuang Nongken	$1,510		Cresud	Agriculture		Argentina	South America		G
2011	June	ICBC	$680	75%	Standard Bank	Finance	Banking	Argentina	South America		
2011	July	Chery Auto	$170		Socma	Transport	Autos	Argentina	South America		G
2011	August	Taiyuan Iron, CITIC, Baosteel	$1,950	15%	CBMM	Metals		Brazil	South America		
2011	August	JAC Motors	$100	20%	SHC	Transport	Autos	Brazil	South America		G
2011	November	CIC	$850	10%	GDF Suez	Energy		Trinidad-Tob	North America		
2011	November	Sinopec	$4,800	30%	Galp Energia	Energy		Brazil	South America		
2011	November	ICBC	$100	5%	Standard Bank	Finance	Banking	Argentina	South America		
2012	February	Xinjiang Goldwind	$190	50%	Mainstream Re	Energy	Alternative	Chile	South America		G
2012	February	Sinochem	$980		Total	Energy	Gas	Colombia	South America		
2012	March	Bosai	$100			Metals	Aluminum	Guyana	South America		
2012	May	State Grid	$940		ACS	Energy		Brazil	South America		
2012	May	China Construction Bank	$200	100%	WestLB	Finance	Banking	Brazil	South America		
2012	June	China Railway Engineering	$118		C.V.G. Ferromir	Metals	Steel	Venezuela	South America		G
2012	September	Xinwei	$300			Technology	Telecom	Nicaragua	North America		G
2012	September	Lenovo	$150	100%	Digibras and Du	Technology		Brazil	South America		
2012	September	Beijing Auto	$300			Transport	Autos	Brazil	South America		G
2012	November	CIC	$460	33%	Prosperitas	Logistics		Brazil	South America		
2013	April	COFCO	$320			Agriculture		Brazil	South America		G
2013	June	Xugong Construction Machinery	$200	100%		Real estate	Constructic	Brazil	South America		G
2013	September	Sinopec	$1,400		Junin 1	Energy	Oil	Venezuela	South America		G
2013	October	CNOOC	$120	10%	Total and Wint	Energy	Gas	Argentina	South America	0	
2013	October	CNOOC and CNPC	$1,400	10%, 10%	Petrobras, Shel	Energy	Oil	Brazil	South America	0	G
2013	October	China Construction Bank	$720	74%	Banco Industria	Finance	Banking	Brazil	South America	0	
2013	November	CNPC	$2,890		Petrobras	Energy		Peru	South America	1	
2013	December	Three Gorges	$130	50%	Cachoeira-caid	Energy	Hydro	Brazil	South America	0	
2013	December	Three Gorges	$250	50%	Jari	Energy	Hydro	Brazil	South America	0	
2014	February	Three Gorges	$390	33%	Terra Novo	Energy	Hydro	Brazil	South America	0	
2014	April	Minmetals, Suzhou Guoxin, and CITIC	$6,990	63, 22, 15%	Glencore	Metals	Copper	Peru	South America	1	G
2014	April	COFCO and Hopu Investment	$750		Noble Agri Limi	Agriculture		Brazil	South America	0	
2014	June	Yida	$740	100%		Tourism		Antigua and	North America	1	G
2014	June	China Railway Construction and China Nonferrous	$2,040		Mirador	Metals	Copper	Ecuador	South America	1	G
2014	July	Sany Heavy	$300	100%		Real estate	Constructic	Brazil	South America	0	G
2014	July	ZTE	$100			Technology	Telecom	Brazil	South America	0	
2014	August	China Construction Bank	$720	72%	Banko Industria	Finance	Banking	Brazil	South America	0	
2014	October	Risen Energy	$230	100%		Energy	Alternative	Mexico	North America	0	G
2014	December	Three Gorges	$140	49%	EDP	Energy	Alternative	Brazil	South America	0	
2015	August	Three Gorges	$490		Triunfo Particip	Energy		Brazil	South America	0	
2015	August	State Construction Engineering	$250			Tourism		Bahamas	North America	0	G
2015	October	ICBC	$2,000		Petrobras	Energy	Oil	Brazil	South America	0	
2015	November	HNA	$460	24%	Azul Linhas Aer	Transport	Aviation	Brazil	South America	0	
2016	January	Three Gorges	$3,660			Energy	Hydro	Brazil	South America	0	
2016	April	State Grid	$110		Mato Grosso	Energy		Brazil	South America	0	

[39]La Nacion (2015), "Costa Rican MPs approve Chinese loan for motorway expansion project", BBC Monitoring Global News IDSA, San Jose , 23 February 2015.

2016	April	China Molybdenum	$1,500		Anglo American	Chemicals		Brazil	South America	0
2016	May	Shanghai Pengxin	$290	57%	Fiagril Participa	Agriculture		Brazil	South America	0
2016	May	Envivsion Energy	$100	50%	Vive Energia	Energy	Alternative	Mexico	North America	0 G
2016	May	Shandong Landbridge	$900			Transport	Shipping	Panama	North America	1
2016	July	Jiquan Iron and Steel	$300	100%	Alumina Partne	Metals		Jamaica	North America	1
2016	July	Xuzhou Construction Machinery	$100			Real estate	Constructic	Brazil	South America	0
2016	September	Chengdu Tianqi	$210	2%	Sociedad Quimi	Metals		Chile	South America	1
2016	September	CIC	$1,090		Petrobras	Energy	Gas	Brazil	South America	0
2016	September	CIC	$410			Energy	Gas	Brazil	South America	0
2016	October	Three Gorges and China Development Bank	$1,200		Duke	Energy		Brazil	South America	0
2016	October	Envision Energy	$290	100%		Energy	Alternative	Argentina	South America	0 G
2016	November	CNPC	$1,460		PDVSA	Energy	Oil	Venezuela	South America	1
2016	November	State Power Investment	$140			Energy	Alternative	Chile	South America	1 G
2016	December	State Grid	$4,910	55%	CPFL	Energy		Brazil	South America	0
2016	December	CNOOC	$1,110			Energy	Oil	Mexico	North America	0 G
2016	December	Didi Chuxing	$100		99Taxis	Transport	Autos	Brazil	South America	0
2017	January	China Communications Construction	$100	80%	Concremat	Real estate	Constructic	Brazil	South America	0
2017	February	JAC Motors	$110		Giant Motors	Transport	Autos	Mexico	North America	0
2017	March	Shougang	$500		Hierro	Metals	Steel	Peru	South America	1
2017	April	Shandong Gold	$960	50%	Barrick	Metals		Argentina	South America	0
2017	April	China Communications Construction	$280	51%		Transport	Shipping	Brazil	South America	0 G
2017	May	BYD	$100	100%		Transport	Autos	Argentina	South America	0 G
2017	June	Shanghai Pengxin	$250		DKBA	Agriculture		Brazil	South America	0
2017	July	CITIC-led fund	$1,100		Dow	Agriculture		Brazil	South America	0
2017	September	China Merchants	$920	90%	TPC	Transport	Shipping	Brazil	South America	0
2017	September	State Power Investment	$2,260			Energy	Hydro	Brazil	South America	0
2017	October	CNPC	$120	20%		Energy	Oil	Brazil	South America	0 G
2017	November	State Grid	$3,440	40%	CPFL	Energy		Brazil	South America	0
2018	January	Southern Power	$1,300	28%	Transelec	Energy		Chile	South America	1
2018	January	Didi Chuxing	$600		99Taxis	Transport	Autos	Brazil	South America	0
2018	April	Three Gorges	$190			Energy	Hydro	Brazil	South America	0
2018	May	China Energy Engineering	$190	100%	Sistema Produt	Utilities		Brazil	South America	0
2018	May	Chengdu Tianqi	$4,070	24%	Sociedad Quimi	Metals		Chile	South America	1
2018	May	CNOOC	$930	25%		Energy	Oil	Guyana	South America	1 G
2018	June	Three Gorges	$240	100%	Cornelio Brenn	Energy	Hydro	Chile	South America	1
2018	June	Chinalco	$1,300			Metals	Copper	Peru	South America	1
2018	July	China Development Bank	$250		PDVSA	Energy	Oil	Venezuela	South America	1 G
2018	July	China Railway Construction	$920		Mirador	Metals	Copper	Ecuador	South America	1
2018	August	Three Gorges	$1,390		Odebrecht	Energy	Hydro	Peru	South America	1
2018	October	Tenecent	$180	5%	Nubank	Finance		Brazil	South America	0
2018	October	Alibaba	$100		StoneCo IPO	Finance		Brazil	South America	0
2018	November	Chinese Academy of Sciences	$830	94%	Australis Seafoc	Agriculture		Chile	South America	1
2018	November	Zhongrong Xinda	$2,360		Pampa de Pong	Metals	Steel	Peru	South America	1
2019	January	China General Nuclear	$780	100%		Energy	Alternative	Brazil	South America	0
2019	January	COSCO	$230	60%	Volcan	Logistics		Peru	South America	1
2019	April	Shangdong Baoma	$250			Transport	Shipping	Uruguay	South America	1
2019	April	Jiangxi Ganfeng Lithium	$160	13%		Metals		Argentina	South America	0
2019	May	China Communications Construction	$220	100%		Metals	Steel	Brazil	South America	0 G

Source: China Global Investment Tracker by American Enterprise Institute

Through its investments and credits China has also assisted the tottering economies of very many LACs to recover. For instance, at one point of time lowering oil prices to approximately 50 dollars per barrel had left the economies of several countries in the region, such as Venezuela in a desperate necessity of financing. In January 2015, the PRC invested more than 20 billion dollars in the faltering Venezuelan economy. Infact between 2010 and 2015, China had offered loans worth than 40 billion dollars to the country, some of which was repaid through oil deliveries.

Since 2014, the Chinese government had instituted three regional funds within the range of $40 to $55 billion in order to support infrastructure as well as other investment projects in

Latin America. The figure below gives an overview of China's regional funds to the LACs.[40]

Table 2: China's Regional Funds

Fund Name	Year Initiated	Amount	Chinese Administrator
China-LAC Cooperation Fund 中拉合作基金	2014	$10–$15 billion	China Export-Import Bank
China-LAC Industrial Cooperation Investment Fund 中拉产能合作投资基金	2015	$20 billion	China Development Bank
Special Loan Program for China-LAC Infrastructure Project 中拉基础设施专项贷款	2015	$10 billion	China Development Bank

Source: Margaret Myers and Kevin Gallagher, "Down but Not Out: Chinese Development Finance in LAC, 2017," *InterAmerican Dialogue and Boston University Global Economic Governance Initiative*, March 2018, 4–5. *https://www.thedialogue.org/wp-content/uploads/2018/03/Chinese-Finance-to-LAC-2017.pdf*

Source: Koleski

Given the above-mentioned statistics and data on Chinese trade and investment in Latin America in general and the individual nations in the region in particular, it can be argued that while the US asserts that it is the "steadiest, strongest, and most enduring partner" of the LACs, it is indeed China which claims and proves that the country pursues a win-win cooperation with the countries in the region, and that its cooperation is founded on principles of reciprocity, equality, inclusiveness and openness.

VIEW OF THE LACS TOWARDS CHINA

A win-win partnership

Within the framework of China's engagement with the LACs as a developing nation, the countries in the region view their

[40]Koleski, Katherine and Alec Blivas (2018), "China's Engagement With Latin America and the Caribbean", [Online: Web] Accessed on 11 December 2018, URL: https://www.uscc.gov/sites/default/files/Research/China%27s%20Engagement%20with%20Latin%20America%20and%20the%20Caribbean_.pdf

engagement with the PRC in general and economic association with the country in particular, as an opportunity. This is very evident from the statements of the leadership of the LACs. For instance, while discussing the overall status of Sino-Guyana bilateral relations David Arthur Granger, the Head of the State of Guyana had said,

> "The Belt and Road initiative is a strong indicator of China's transformative vision for the world. Guyana signed a Memorandum of Understanding to cooperate within the framework of the Initiative. We welcome increased Chinese investment. We are committed to ensuring a safe and secure environment for all investors. International environmental cooperation, in the context of the threats posed by climate change and natural disasters, is an urgent necessity. We look forward to learning from China's experience in protecting the environment and in mitigating the adverse effects of climate change. Guyana and China have much to celebrate".[41]

A remarkable characteristic of Chinese engagement with the LACs is the degree of respect and importance that the Asian giant has ascribed to these nations, from time to time. This stands in sharp contrast to the US approach of disdain toward the region. Such relations of cordiality have drawn the LACs towards China. Not only do the countries in the region revere the Chinese model of development but also hail the opening up reforms of Beijing, as it presents them with enough scope to diversify their exports.

[41]Ministry of the Presidency Cooperative Republic of Guyana (2018), "Guyana and China share a common desire to strengthen economic relations and trade –President Granger", [Online: Web] Accessed on 12 December 2018, URL: https://motp.gov.gy/index.php/2015-07-20-18-49-38/2015-07-20-18-50-14/3207-guyana-and-china-share-a-common-desire-to-strengthen-economic-relations-andtrade-president-granger.

The leaders of the LACs also acknowledge the vibrant economic complementarity in their relationship with China. In 2016, the then newly appointed Argentinean ambassador to China described the country's association with the PRC as an "enormous opportunity" to boost as well as diversify its exports. As of 2016, Ambassador Guelar noted that approximately 86 percent of the country's exports to Beijing comprised of food products sold by as many as 15 big companies, while 99 percent of what China exports to Argentina are industrial commodities from some 3000 enterprises. President Mauricio Macri of Argentina had once mentioned with refercnce to China that, "We have complementary countries. There are few countries in the world that can buy so many of the high-quality products that we're capable of making".[42]

Infact China and Argentina share a comprehensive strategic partnership and China is engaged in a number of bilateral projects in the country, such as modernization of Belgrano Cargas cargo railway as well as energy and mining cooperation. In this regard, Ambassador Guelar had said, "We don't view China as a lifesaver, but as an element for Argentina's development". Also given the fact that Renminbi, the Chinese currency has been included in the Special Drawing Rights (SDR) basket of the IMF, the country's global presence has definitely got cemented.[43]

Countries in the region seek to bolster their economic engagement with the country. For instance, way back in 2014, former Venezuelan President Nicolas Maduro proclaimed the

[42]VOA News (2018), "Argentina, China Sign Deals Strengthening Ties After G-20", [Online: Web] Accessed on December 13, 2018, URL: https://www.voanews.com/americas/argentina-china-sign-deals-strengthening-tiesafter-g-20.

[43]Xinhua (2016), "Argentine envoy says China offers "enormous opportunity" for developing nations", Buenos Aires, 22 February 2016.

decision to institute a special economic zone to usher in Chinese manufacturing enterprises of machinery as well as supplies for construction, which as he mentioned would later be accessible to enterprises from other nations. On this occasion he said,

> "I want Chinese entrepreneurs to know that we are going to install a special economic zone in two places in the country (Central and East) to install all these investments there in special conditions that attract the direct investment of Chinese enterprises in the first place and it will be open to all who want to come to invest".[44]

Such an urge to cooperate with China is to the extent that leaderships in the LACs have very often reiterated that irrespective of the political party in power, the successive governments of these nations would continue to maintain relations of goodwill and bonhomie with China. For instance, former Argentine Foreign Minister Hector Timerman had once mentioned that irrespective of the leader in power "Argentina will continue to pursue a friendly policy toward China".[45]

The Chinese model of economic growth has inspired very many countries in the region. Costa Rica is one such case. Motivated by a Chinese model that was introduced way back in the 1980s, Costa Rica had entered into an accord with the PRC to commence work on a special economic zone (SEZ) in its territory. The project of the SEZ in the South American country sought to stimulate the less developed geographic region by attracting more investment. The two countries had also signed a protocol that

[44]El Mundo (2014), "Venezuela to create special economic zone for Chinese factories", BBC Monitoring Global News IDSA, Caracas , 21 September 2014.

[45]Xinhua (2015a), "New Argentine government keen on closer ties with China", BBC Monitoring Global News IDSA, Beijing, 08 December 2015.

sought to export Costa Rican prawns to the promising Chinese market, a huge consumer of this seafood.[46]

With regard to the rising bonhomie between China and the LACs, Xie Tao, professor of international studies at the Beijing Foreign Studies University, mentioned that :

> "China's economic influence there is largely driven by China's need for resources, and such influence is not sustainable" and "the countries there are less suspicious of China because they know that the US is in the vicinity".[47]

While discussing China's engagement with Latin America, a passing reference of Sino-US contestation in the region deserves mention. In this regard, it may be stated that there is a rising trend amongst the governments of the LACs to favour closer engagement with China over and above the US. The ALBA bloc deserves reference here. The ALBA bloc in the region, which came into existence in the twenty first century, seeks to decrease the region's long-standing dependence on Western aid by elevating intra-regional partnership and collaboration in certain chief sectors namely trade and energy. The bloc was founded in 2004 initially by Hugo Chavez of Venezuela and Fidel Castro of Cuba[48]. However, it now comprises of Bolivia, Antigua and Barbuda, Dominica, Cuba, Nicaragua, Grenada, Saint Lucia, Federation of Saint Kitts and Nevis, Saint Vincent and the Grenadines,

[46]Prensa, Libre(2015), "Costa Rica, China sign strategic partnership agreement", BBC Monitoring Global News IDSA, San Jose, 6 January 2015.

[47] Ng, Teddy and Victoria Ruan and Lawrence Chung (2015), "Beijing to host Latin America delegation in bid to flex muscles on doorstep of US", [Online: Web] Accessed on 13 November 2018, URL: https://www.scmp.com/news/china/article/1675912/latin-america-comes-beijing-firstcooperation-forum

[48]ALBA Info, "Information on The Bolivarian Alliance", [Online: Web] Accessed on 12August 2019, URL: https://albainfo.org/what-is-the-alba/

Venezuela and Ecuador.[49] It is this diplomatic posture of the bloc that makes it a desirable diplomatic partner for the PRC.[50]

Apart from the ALBA nations, other countries in the region too have demonstrated intent to engage more closely with China vis-à-vis the US. This is visible in Argentine lawmaker Carlos Raimundi's statement, "The United States and its dollar no longer represent absolute hegemony over the planet" and that "thanks to the accords with China, the panorama for the people of Argentina is very promising, as they affirm an independent path" towards the advancement of the country. He further mentioned that the Chinese style of instituting ties "is not one of subjugation, of destabilization, of funding coups against governments under a different system, but of accords that respect the sovereignty of each country".[51]

The reason for the development of such sentiments of goodwill is also the relentless Chinese expression of support towards the region, unlike the US. For instance, in 2016 President Xi Jinping delivered a speech at the Peruvian Congress, where he mentioned,

> "All countries are equal members of the international community. The big, strong and rich must not bully the small, weak and poor. And the right of every country to independently choose its social system and development

[49]Xinhua (2018), "ALBA bloc vows to defend peace in Latin America, Caribbean", [Online: Web] Accessed on 12 August 2019, URL: http://www.xinhuanet.com/english/2018-12/15/c_137676372.htm

[50]Kramer, Andrew (2019), "In Latin America, the Price of U.S. Neglect is High", [Online: Web] Accessed on 12 August 2019, URL: https://www.usni.org/magazines/proceedings/2019/june/latin-america-price-usneglect-high.

[51]Xinhua (2015i), "Argentina lawmaker welcomes pacts signed with China", BBC Monitoring Global News IDSA, Beijing, 6 February 2015.

path should be upheld" and "With one fifth of the world's total area and nearly one third of the world's population, China and Latin America and the Caribbean are crucial forces for world peace and stability".[52]

On various instances, China has also acted as a responsible stakeholder in the region. A case in point is the PRC's stand on the peace process in Colombia. The peace process in Colombia has been underway since 2012 between the formerly biggest guerrilla group – Revolutionary Armed Forces of Colombia (FARC) – and the Colombian government. It seeks to conclude a domestic armed conflict, which has been in place for over fifty years now. In February 2017, official peace talks commenced between the Colombian Government and the National Liberation Army (ELN), the guerrilla group. The PRC, on its part, has proclaimed support for the cause and holds the position that such a peace process is not only critical for the stability of the nation but also the region at large (XinhuaNet 2019d).[53]

While discussing the high points of China's engagement with the LACs, it is important to state that owing to splendid trade relations between the two sides, influx of massive Chinese investment in the region and cooperation between the PRC and the LACs on a range of issues, China has evolved as an attractive partner for the countries in the region. It is the financial aspect, which is at the heart of such an engagement. Since the LACs – that maintain diplomatic relations with the PRC – have been

[52]People's Daily (2016), "Quotable quotes from President Xi's speech at Peruvian Congress", [Online: Web] Accessed on 11 August 2019, URL: http://en.people.cn/n3/2016/1122/c90000-9145336.html

[53]XinhuaNet (2019d), "Chinese envoy says Colombian peace process matters for region", [Online: Web] Accessed on 11 August 2019, URL: http://www.*Xinhuanet.com/english/2019-07/20/c_138241579.htm

greatly benefitted commercially leading to their overall socio-economic development and sustenance of many of their faltering economies, the remaining countries in the region have begun to view the Asian giant as favourable prospect. Consequently, there has been a trend of the LACs 'breaking' off ties with ROC and switching their allegiance towards the PRC.

In one such case, when the Dominican Republic switched ties to formally recognise the PRC, Wang Kung-yi, professor of political science at Chinese Culture University in Taipei said, "Beijing has become more and more sophisticated in playing the money diplomacy game" and in "this way, Beijing has not only won the support of the government, but also those from the public, which would mean a big deal in terms of wrestling with Washington."[54]

The Pessimistic Aspect of the Relationship

Having discussed the high-points of Sino-Latin American engagement, it is also important to bring to light the pessimistic viewpoints and the risks comprising Chinese inroads that have been doing the rounds within the region as well as outside.

First, there is clearly a visible trend of slowing down of China's GDP from a double-digit rate as was common in the previous decades to a more moderate IMF estimate of 6-8 percent annually. This leads to the obvious risk of China cooling down as a market. Apart from the volatility of markets that a slower growth rate might bring about, the trend of China becoming an export

[54]Wong, Catherine (2018), "Why China hopes Taiwan losing the support of a tiny Caribbean country will send a message to the US", [Online: Web] Accessed on 11 August 2019, URL: https://www.businessinsider.com/dominican-republicrecognizing-china-over-taiwan-to-send-message-to-us-2018-5?IR=T.

market for the region's products, would leave a deep environmental footprint and little employment benefit for the local populace. This is primarily because the overall Sino-Latin American trade levies great pressure on the region by generating more greenhouse gas, using more water and creating only few jobs.

Second, apart from environmental hazards, there have been numerous instances when Chinese enterprises have been criticised for not respecting the rights of workers in the LACs.

For example, Wills Rangel, president of Bolivarian Socialist Workers' Federation (CBST) voiced his opinion about the necessity of companies working in the Orinoco Oil Belt, especially those from China and Russia, to adhere to Venezuelan laws and respect the rights of workers.

He said,

> "There have been many complaints from oil workers at all levels. It is noted that the Chinese company CNPC and Russian companies Gazprom, Lukoil, and Rosneft do not respect workers' rights under the Labour Law. In most contracts benefits are not provided, forming unions is banned, and collective agreements are not allowed; there is even the use of piecework to avoid paying the legal benefits".[55]

Third, another risk comprises the asymmetric nature of Sino-Latin American trade. China is not simply importing every kind of commodity from the LACs. Infact, the surge in China's imports primarily account for the strategically important raw materials such as soybeans and petroleum. This fresh focus essentially originates from two of China's recent policy shifts.

[55]El Mundo (2015), "Venezuelan oil workers demand that Chinese, Russian companies honour contracts", BBC Monitoring Global News IDSA, Caracas, 1 April 2015.

The first is the "Go Out" policy, which has been pushing Chinese enterprises to invest outside the country since 1999. The second policy refers to the "Two Markets, Two Resources" policy to food security. This strategy distinguishes between the strategic staples that the country could produce in adequate capacity at home, and those that the country needs to continue to import from outside. In this context, it maybe stated that the import of the LACs from Beijing has also witnessed a steady rise. These imports mainly comprise of finished goods.

University professor Felix Arellano has said that Beijing's approach towards the region is that of vending out manufactured goods and purchasing raw materials. Taking the case of Venezuela he said, "In Venezuela the business relationship has been intensified by the destruction of the productive apparatus and the high rates of inflation and shortages."[56]

Fourth, is the issue of declining rate of employment generation in the region. One aspect to the issue is that manufacturing creates greater percentage of job generation as compared to cultivation, extraction and production of primary commodities. Thus, the constitution of raw materials as key component of Sino-Latin American trade gives rise to a form of commercial exchange that supports lesser job generation opportunities for the local masses .[57] As an example to this end, the cases of St Lucia and Guyana maybe stated. In the recent years, the St Lucia Manufacturers Association (SLMA) in St

[56]El Nacional (2014), "Venezuelan daily points to aspects not announced in agreements with China", BBC Monitoring Global News IDSA, Caracas, 22 July 2014.

[57]Ray, Rebecca (2014), "Latin America's Risky China Boom", [Online:Web] Accessed 15 July 2016, URL: https://nacla.org/article/latin-america%E2%80%99s-risky-chinaboom.

Lucia has voiced their concern regarding the increasing influx of Chinese nationals in the East Caribbean region. The SLMA had registered a concern on this matter with Organization of Eastern Caribbean States (OECS).

In this regard, Paula Calderon, SLMA president had reached out to the OECS leaders to mention,

> "When they (Chinese nationals) come into the country if they want to invest in a particular area, then they must employ a certain number of people, and they must pass on a certain level of training to those they employ. These should be among the rules and regulations that we need to mandate to ensure that our people are protected."[58]

However, against such concerns of the local manufacturers in the LACs, the government of these nations have tried to adhere to a middle ground approach. For instance, responding to the concerns of the SLMA president, the then foreign minister of St Lucia, had said that instead of aiding them with protection, the existing government would strive to make the local entrepreneurs more competitive.[59]

The other example is that of Guyana. Over the last decade, there has been a rise in the PRC's interest in the natural resources of Guyana. This has led to several Guyanese citizens to doubt the value of their country's apparently equal partnership with China. An instance to this end is the controversial investment plans of Chinese enterprise Bai Shan Lin in Guyana. The Bai Shan Lin

[58]Caribbean Media Corporation (2012a), "St Lucia manufacturers want sub-regional leaders to deal with Chinese influx", BBC Monitoring Global News IDSA, Bridgetown, 30 January 2012.

[59]Caribbean Media Corporation (2012b), "St Lucia's minister pledges help not protection from Chinese businesses influx", BBC Monitoring Global News IDSA, Bridgetown, 6 February 2012.

enterprise was awarded a forestry concession that comprised of approximately one million hectares of rainforest, from where the company would harvest logs and ship them out of the South American country. Over and above the acquisition of important land holdings, the enterprise had proclaimed the formation of a 400-acre "Bai Shan Lin Real Estate Development Project" as well as an extensive "Guyana-China Timber Industry Economic & Trading Cooperation Park". While the Chinese investment in this country has been indeed huge, there was much apprehension that such a project would be of little benefit to the local people of the country, outside of the political circles, owing to the trend of the Chinese enterprises to bring in their own labour in order to staff operations in Guyana.

In another case in the country, while many local people continued to remain in need of work or underemployed, Chinese workers were imported to build the Marriott Hotel in Georgetown in early 2013. These incidents have given rise to massive criticism against the surge in Chinese investment in the country's growing mining and forestry sectors. To this end, the political opposition in Guyana has demanded greater transparency in the investment agreements between Bai Shan Lin and the Guyanese government, whereby the details of the accord would be made public.[60]

Fifth, is the concern that the increasing influx of Chinese goods have led to displacement of traditional manufacturers in the Latin American markets. For instance, in 2011 Luis Gustavo Florez, the president of the Colombian Industrialists' Association of Shoe, Leather, and Manufactured Articles (ACICAM) had

[60]Edwards, Kevin (2013), "Guyana: Colonialism With Chinese Characteristics?", [Online: Web] Accessed on 12 December 2018, URL: https://nacla.org/blog/2013/6/26/guyana-colonialism-chinese-characteristics.

stated that illegal procurements from the PRC was a prime cause for the decline in the sale of locally produced goods as well as employment rate in the leather sector. He said, "Colombian production at present supplies only 53 per cent of the local market. But technical contraband and under-invoicing for Chinese products has blown a hole in the market of almost 120 billion pesos [63,660,553 dollars at current rate of exchange]". The metalworking division also witnessed a similar situation. Imports from the PRC for Colombia's production chain hiked from 128 million dollars in 2001 to 1.772 billion dollars in 2010.[61]

In this regard, Guillermo Moreno, director of the Latin American Steel Association (ALACERO) stated:

> "The price of scrap metal exported to China is higher than that of a number of imported iron and steel products. This situation directly affects employment and sales in regional industry, which has to eliminate highly-skilled jobs in order to survive on account of products made from the raw materials".[62]

Sixth is the issue of lack of transparency in the accords signed by the Chinese government with the respective governments of the LACs. This has very often led to the governments of the LACs facing severe criticism from their opposition parties. Interestingly, in these situations governments of the LACs have adhered to a stern pro-China stand. For instance, in 2012 the Antigua and Barbuda government led by United Progressive Party (UPP) administration had faced flak from its opposition party for the above-mentioned reason. However, in response to such criticism, on the occasion of Beijing delivering a multi-million dollar project of a community centre to the government of Barbuda, the then

[61] El Espectador (2012), "Colombian paper says Chinese imports harming local industry", BBC Monitoring Global News IDSA, Bogota, 04 January 2012.

[62] *Ibid*

Prime Minister Baldwin Spencer commented on the status of Sino-Antigua and Barbuda relations:

> "I wish to assure you the people of Barbuda and Antigua that the relationship between the United Progressive Party administration and the People's Republic of China is here to stay and there are many more projects to come – all in the interest of you the people of Barbuda and Antigua."[63]

He further stated:

"The attacks on the relationship between Antigua and Barbuda and the People's Republic of China in some quarters of the opposition and the media are unpatriotic and dangerous and are designed to........ derail the progress of the relationship between the United Progressive Party Administration and the People's Republic of China".[64]

Alongside the issue of lack of transparency in Sino-Latin American agreements, there is another associated issue of corruption and non-transparency within the governments of the LACs itself. For instance, the Venezuelan government under the Hugo Chavez administration had been subjected to criticism owing to the lack of transparency in the management of funds. In 2012, on the occasion of Chinese funds worth 22 billion dollars being transferred to the Venezuelan Bank for Economic and Social Development, there were public denunciations with regard to the clarity of the manner in which the money was being handled by the National Executive. Doubting these money handlings, former opposition deputy Miguel Angel Rodriguez had even questioned the productivity condition of Venezuela, the condition of water service and electrical energy generation, the state of national

[63]Caribbean Media Corporation (2012c), "Antiguan premier defends relationship with China", BBC Monitoring Global News IDSA, Bridgetown, 20 January 2012.

[64]Official Website of Government of Antigua and Barbuda (2012), "Chinese Government Hands Over Multi-Million Dollar Community Centre To Barbuda", [Online: Web] Accessed on February 13, 2018, URL: http://solidwaste.gov.ag/article_details.php?id=2488&category=38

infrastructure as well as shortage of housing facilities. In other words, Rodriguez emphasised that the prominent investments did not feature in the Venezuelan reality and consequently questioned the transparency of money handling by the government.[65]

CHINESE INROAD INTO THE REGION: CONCLUDING REMARKS

At present, China has diplomatic relations with as many as 24 nations in the region of Latin America. This is definitely a significant number for the region to weigh high on China's foreign policy agenda. Clearly, the country's economic diplomacy enables it to institutionalize its engagement in Latin America and amass support in the international realm.

The country has maintained a cautious stance of not making the US wary of its growing proximity with the LACs. In the White Paper on Latin America and the Caribbean issued in 2016, the Chinese government has specifically mentioned that China seeks to bolster military cooperation with the LAC, which however is not aimed at targeting or excluding "any third party". Although China has not named US per se, but the phrase "third party" is most likely directed towards the country.

The principal argument of this work is that China's inroads in the region is driven by its economic objectives over and above its strategic considerations. As has been discussed previously in this work, economic development is critical for China at the present moment. So as to gain recognition as a key economic player in the international sphere and to shape the rules of global governance, it is imperative that China is economically strong from within. To this end, Latin America is of key importance to the country. Apart from seeking raw materials from these resource rich nations, Beijing also seeks to diversify the source of imports and gain hold of a secure market for its manufactured products. To add to it,

[65]El Universal (2012), "Venezuelan minister says oil exports to China to reach 1m barrels by 2015", BBC Monitoring Global News IDSA, Caracas , 9 February 2012.

countries like Venezuela and Brazil satiate China's quest for energy security.

To add to it, China and the LACs have a shared stance of instituting a multipolar world order in which the hegemonic influence of a few big powers could be curbed. Also such a world system would grant the developing world a greater voice to express their views, opinions and challenges. In line with this objective, the PRC as well as the LACs demand reformation of the institutions of global governance to reallocate institutional influence and shape the decision-making structures of these bodies in a manner that they would conform to the realities of the twenty first century. China also seeks a network of allies in the developing world to ward off Western criticism towards it on issues of human rights, Taiwan and the like. In order to draw these objectives, China has used economic diplomacy to draw the LACs towards it. This comprises of means such as offering various kinds of loans, making greater investment in the economies of the LACs, bolstering trade, offering aid, and cash infusion for infrastructure development of these countries.

The other objective of China in Latin America is to isolate the ROC in the region. While China has diplomatic ties with 24 nations in the region, Taiwan has official relations with only 9 countries at present. The region is equally important for Taiwan, as out of 16 diplomatic partners worldwide, 9 are from the region of South America. Both China as well as Taiwan have utilized the tactic of offering economic assistance to these nations to lure their support. Such economic diplomacy is often termed as "checkbook" diplomacy. Undoubtedly, its effect is visible, as Panama, the Dominican Republic and El Salvador have switched sides in 2017 and 2018. They have now officially established diplomatic relations with the PRC. In a way, China has pursued economic diplomacy to accomplish its economic objectives in the region, which has drawn the remaining LAC towards it. Thus, through the means of fulfilling its economic objectives, China is also attaining its strategic objectives in the region.

A glowing reason for China's growing proximity with the countries in the region is also the shift in the interest of the Latin American leadership in instituting closer ties with Beijing. From once being apprehensive of Chinese designs owing to ignorance of each other's culture, the turn of the century has witnessed a fresh beginning of the relationship. The LACs now seek to re-shape their economies in accordance to the Chinese model of development; earn greater infrastructure investments from Beijing; reap the benefits of the One Belt One Road initiative that would facilitate it with greater connectivity to the outer world; expand the choice of its trading partners, diversify the source of import, multiplying the markets of export thereby reducing reliance on the US; and secure the support of China in reforming the existing institutions of global governance, which would consequently give it a greater voice in setting the norms of global economic and political governance in the world. Not only has China brought with it, a market of 1.3 billion consumers, but also investment, infrastructure development as well as sufficient scope of employment generation in these countries. Therefore, the dragon has successfully ingressed into the region and emerged as a favoured nation amongst the LACs.

(Dr Shaheli Das is a Sinologist and has been a researcher in several premier think tanks in India and abroad. She has written columns and articles for forums such as Forbes, the Diplomat, BRICS Post and Financial Express. She can be reached at shaheli02@gmail.com)

Chapter 12

China's Strategic Interests in Africa

– Dr. Abhishek Darbey

China is planning as well as working for a long term strategic roles to play in Africa. At present, China's activities as well as actions in Africa are basically directed at their strategic interests and longer term goals. Under the ambitious project Belt & Road initiative, China is investing heavily in Africa to build this continent suitable for their ways of doing trade to fulfil their economic agendas supported by hard muscle power to sustain their presence as well as interests in the continent. For few reasons, Africa becomes an appropriate choice for China, first, the continent is a rich source of mineral resources; second, geo-strategically as well as geo-politically, Africa is always significant for any major power with great ambitions to become a superpower or a global power; third, Africa will be a better market for any economy dominating the consumer markets with its cheaper products.

Collectively, the countries of Africa would need to spend US$130-170 billion per year to meet their infrastructure needs, but, according to African Development Bank, Africa is getting short of amount US$68-US$108 billion every year of the total needs.[1] This gap in infrastructure investment in Africa creates an opportunity for China. China is fuelling its economic growth, expanding its logistics footprint sharpening its political influence in multilateral forums.[2] China is now Africa's biggest trade partner, with Sino-Africa trade volume of US200 billion per year. According to Mckinsey, over 10,000 China owned firms are currently operating throughout the African continent, and the value of Chinese business there since 2005 amounts to more than US$2 trillion, with US$300 billion in investment currently on the table.[3] Infrastructure is what Africa needs most and infrastructure is what China is most equipped to provide. Many African leaders are looking to China to bring their experience to their countries. Since 2011, China has been the biggest player in Africa's infrastructure field, claiming a 40% share that continues to rise. Meanwhile, the share of other players are falling precipitously, Europe declined from 44% to 34%, while the presence of the US contractors fell from 24% to just 6.7%. Under the Belt & Road Initiative (BRI), Africa is realising inland, hinterland, and coastal connectivity by creating economic corridors for land, sea and air transportation routes. The improvement of Africa's logistics system will enhance the efficiency of its export capacity and reduce product transportation costs, and lastly, it will promote intra-regional and global trade.[4]

[1]"Africa's' Infrastructure: Great Potential but Little Impact on Inclusive Growth" https://www.afdb.org/fileadmin/uploads/afdb/ Documents/ Publications/2018AEO/African_Economic_Outlook_2018_-_EN_Chapter3.pdf

[2]*Ibid.*

[3]'According to Mckinsey, over 10,000 China owned firms are currently operating throughout the African continent', https://www.forbes.com/ sites/wadeshepard/2019/10/03/what-china-is-really-up-to-in-africa/?sh= 4f9bcd8b5930

[4]*Ibid.*

Africa fits into China's grand strategy because Africa is a strategic node in the maritime portion of the BRI i.e. the 21st Century Maritime Silk Road (MSR) that links China to East Africa, Southeast Asia, the Persian Gulf and Europe and recently the MSR is extended to west and southern Africa.[5] Also, the continent has more than 10% of global oil reserves and 7.5% of global natural resources, and China seeks both greater supply and greater diversity of supplies in the context of rapid demand growth. Chinese consortium, engineering and resource firms have sought to expand into African markets.[6]

CHINA'S INFRASTRUCTURE PROJECTS IN AFRICA

Among the ongoing Chinese projects in Africa, 160 projects were undertaken by Chinese enterprises which accounts for 33.2% of the total projects in Africa, and these projects are mainly concentrated in the transportation industry. In terms of project financing, 91 projects were funded by China accounting for 18.8 % of total Chinese projects. In East Africa, China's construction projects accounted for 54.7% and financing projects accounted for 25.9%.[7]

Djibouti

Major Chinese projects are Addis-Ababa- Djibouti Railways and Ethiopia-Djibouti water pipeline. Doraleh Multi-purpose Port,

[5] *Ibid*.

[6] Lloyd Thrall, "China's Expanding African Relations: Implications for U.S. National Security", 2015; Publisher: RAND Corporation https://www.jstor.org/stable/10.7249/j.ctt15zc655.9?seq=1#metadata_info_tab_contents.

[7] Hannah Marais & Jean-Pierre Labuschagne, "If you want to prosper, consider building roads : China's role in African infrastructure and capital projects" 22 March 2019, *Deloitte* https://www2.deloitte.com/us/en/insights/industry/public-sector/china-investment-africa-infrastructure-development.html.

the Hassan Gouled Aptidon International Airport on Obock was built with financial support of US$596 from China. In total, the EXIM Bank of China lent approximately US1 billion to Djibouti funding nearly 40% of Djibouti's substantial infrastructure and investment project.[8]

Egypt

In Egypt, the major Chinese projects include Chinese Industrial Zone in the Gulf of Suez; an Electric Train System for its new Capital. From 2015-2017, Egypt borrowed US1.03 billion from China to finance various infrastructure projects. In 2018, a Chinese consortium that included Shanghai Electric and Dongfang Electric won a tender for a 6,000 MW coal fired electricity generating plant in El-Hamrawein harbor on the Red Sea with a bid of US$4.4 billion.[9]

Ethiopia

In Ethiopia, the major Chinese projects are: Construction of a new electric standard gauge Addis Ababa -Djibouti Railways.[10]

Kenya

The Mombasa-Nairobi Standard Gauge Railway connecting Mombasa to Nairobi was completed and inaugurated on May 31, 2017 and it was built and is operated by the Chinese companies. The total cost of this project is US$ 3.6 Billion.[11]

[8]List of projects of the Belt and Road Initiative https://en.wikipedia.org/wiki/List_of_projects_of_the_Belt_and_Road_Initiative.

[9]*Ibid.*

[10]*Ibid.*

[11]*Ibid.*

Nigeria

Abuja-Kaduna Railway project of Nigeria was completed in 2014 but was opened to the traffic in July 2016 and it was built by China Civil Engineering Construction Company (CCECC) at the estimated cost of US$874 and the China EXIM Bank provided US$500 million concessional loans for the project.[12]

Sudan

Chinese companies has helped Sudan in establishing oil industry and provided agricultural assistance for the cotton industry. China's future infrastructure building plan in the country include railway, roads, ports, nuclear power station, solar power plant and more dams for irrigation and electricity generation.

Uganda

In Uganda, China has financed two major hydro-electricity projects are: The Karuma Hydropower Project and Isimba Hydroelectric Power Station. The EXIM Bank of China has covered 85% of the total cost of these two projects. China has also financed US$350 million to build Entebbe-Kampala Expressway.[13] In 2020, China has announced US$118 million for roads, which is part of an oil production project.

Algeria

Deep water Port in Algeria was constructed by a China-Algeria consortium of companies such as CHEC, CSEC and Algeria's

[12] *Ibid*.

[13] Entebbe–Kampala Expressway https://en.wikipedia.org/wiki/Entebbe%E2%80%93Kampala_Expressway.

Public Port Service Group. The port is connected to Algerian Railway lines and east-west highway, which is one of Algeria's main land based transport networks, and even this highway was constructed by a Chinese consortium composed of CITIC Corporation and China Railway Construction Corporation (CRCC).[14]

Eritrea

The Eritrean Government and the Chinese construction company China SFRCO Group have launched the 1st phase of the Adi- Guadad- Akordet road infrastructure project that features a two lane 134 km new asphalt road.[15]

CHINESE INVESTED/BUILT SEAPORTS IN AFRICA

A total of 46 Sub-Saharan Africa Ports with financial, construction or operational involvement by the Chinese entities have been reported. The Sub-Saharan Africa ports play an integral role in China's Belt & Road Initiative (BRI) and these ports are the backbone of the Maritime Silk Road (MSR). There are three stages of the Chinese infrastructure projects in Africa, first, enabling Beijing to potentially restrict access to its rivals; second, exploit ports during conflict; and third, collect intelligence. The investments in African ports provide a gateway to the region's trade and economic development and will also empower China with political leverage and clout on the continent. These ports will provide a foothold for Plan Navy

[14]*Ibid.*

[15]Mu Xuequan, "Eritrea launches first phase of Chinese-contracted road project" *Xinhua*, 13 November 2013. http://www.xinhuanet.com/english/2019-11/13/c_138552629.htm.

activities and will achieve Chinese military, commercial and political objectives.

At least six of the 46 ports were visited by the Chinese naval vessels or are dual use civil and military ports. 7 out of the 11 ports operated by the Chinese entities are deep water port and thereby opening the possibility for larger commercial and military vessels. The Chinese investment is 17% of the 172 Sub-Saharan Africa Ports are positioned along each coast providing China access to main maritime route and check points. Chinese entities operate 11 of the 46 SSA ports identified so far and among them 7 are on west coast and 4 on the east coast. Chinese entities have financed 27 of the 46 SSA ports and operate 75% of the Chinese financed ports. Chinese entities have constructed 90% of these ports and have overseen construction projects at 41 of the 46 ports in the SSA.

Ports in SSA Operated by Chinese Entities are:

West Africa

- Lekki Deep Sea Port in Lagos, Nigeria
- Tonkolili Ore Project, Pepel Port & Tagrin Point Port in Pepel, Sierra Leone
- Kribi Container Terminal, Kribi Deep Sea Port in Mboro Vilalge (Kribi) Cameroon
- Various Projects, Autonomous Port of Abidjan in Abidjan, Cote d'Ivoire
- Tin-Can Island Port Container Terminal Limited, Tin Can Island Port in Tin Can Island (Lagos), Nigeria
- Lome Container Terminal, Lome Port in Lome, Togo

East Africa

- Doraleh Multipurpose Port, Port of Djibouti in Djibouti City, Djibouti

- Bagamoyo Port in Bagamoyo, Tanzania
- Maruhubi Multipurpose Port in Mpiga-Duri, Tanzania
- Shaikh Ibrahim Livestock Pier, Port of Sudan in Port Sudan, Sudan

Central Africa

- Pointe Noire Mineral (Ore) Port Project, Port of Pointe Noire in Pointe-Noire, Republic of the Congo

PORTS FINANCED OR CONSTRUCTED BY CHINESE ENTITIES

West Africa

- Conakry Container Wharf Expansion Project, Port of Conakry in Conakry, Guinea
- Various Expansion Project, Friendship Port of Nouakchott in Nouakchott, Mauritania
- Tema LNG Terminal, Tema Port in Tema, Ghana
- Takoradi Port in Takoradi, Ghana
- Bakassi Deep Sea Port in Calabar, Nigeria
- Multipurpose Terminal Project, Apapa Port in Apapa (Lagos), Nigeria
- Mindelo Deepwater Port in Mindelo, Cabo Verde
- Kamsar Fishing Port Economic Zone in Kamsar, Guinea
- Mineral Port of Nouadhibou in Nouadhibou, Mauritania
- Atuabo Free Port in Atuabo, Ghana
- Queen Elizabeth II Quay Expansion Project, Freetown Port in Freetown, Sierra Leone
- Douala Chanel Expansion Project, Douala Port in Douala, Cameroon
- Jamestown Fishing Port Complex in Jamestown (Accara),

Ghana

- Simandou Iron Ore Project, Makatong Deep Water Port in Matakong, Guinea

PORTS FINANCED OR CONSTRUCTED BY CHINESE ENTITIES

East Africa

- Tadjourah Port in Tadjourah, Djibouti
- Djibouti Damerjog Industries Development in Damerjog, Djibouti
- Various Expansion Projects, Dar es Salaam Port in dar es Salaam, Tanzania
- Expansion Project, Ntwara Port in Mtwara, Tanzania
- Various Expansion Projects, Massawa New Port in Massawa, Eritrea
- Lamu Port in Lamu, Kenya
- Construction of Three Berths, Mombasa Port in Mombasa, kenya

Central Africa

- Expansion and Rehabilitation Project, Port of Bata in bata, Equatorial Guinea
- Deep Sea Trans-Shipment Port in Fernao Dias in Sao Tome e Principe
- Various Expansion Projects, Port Mole in Libreville, Gabon

PORTS FINANCED OR CONSTRUCTED BY CHINESE ENTITIES

Southern Africa

- Various Expansion Projects, Port of Mobito in Lobiti, ANgola
- Caio Deep Water Port in Caio, ANgola
- Rehabiliation and Expansion Project, Beira Fishing Port in Durban, South Africa
- Various Renovation Projects, Port of Ambodifotatra in

Ambodifotatra (Nosy Boraha), Madagascar

- Tamatave Deepwater Harbour in Toamasina, Madagascar
- Narinda Bay Deep-water Port in bay of Narinda, Madagascar
- Various Expansion Projects, Port of Walvis Bay in Walvis Bay, Namibia
- Port of Cabinda in Cabinda, Angola
- Shipbuilding and Repair Facility, Richards Bay Port in Richard Bay, South Africa
- Deep Water Port of Techobanine in Matutuine District (Maputo), Mozambique

There are 33 coastal countries on the African continent. The countries that China did not participate in port construction on the African continent are: South Africa, Gabon, Benin, Liberia, Guinea-Bissau, Senegal, Gambia, Western Sahara, Morocco, Tunisia, Libya, Eritrea, Somalia and other 13 countries. (Mainly Northwest African countries and North African countries)

CHINA'S DIGITAL SILK ROAD IN AFRICA: PEACE SOUTH

The *PEACE South* cable will connect Djibouti and Kenya to Ethiopia, Uganda, Zambia, Congo and even to the west coast of Africa through territorial cable in Africa, which is termed as PEACE South. In January 20, 2020, it was reported that the PCCW Global and PEACE Cable International Network Co., Ltd. will collaborate on extending the Pakistan East Africa Connecting Europe (PEACE) submarine cable system to

[16]Jason McGee-Abe, "PCCW Global signs up to extend PEACE cable to southern Africa", *Capacity Media,* 20 January 2020 . https://www.capacitymedia.com/articles/3824785/pccw-global-signs-up-to-extend-peace-cable-to-southern-africa.

southern Africa.[16] The PEACE South extension will boost bandwidth and it will connect the current Africa landing point in Mombasa, Kenya all the way to South Africa. It will connect southern Africa to Europe and Asia with faster, newer high bandwidth technology. It will improve the internet usage in the region and reduce the cost of connectivity. "The planned extension through the PEACE South is a natural expansion for Asian Investment in Africa, enhancing cooperation and shared economic benefits in the exchange of goods, technology and ideas. In September 2020, the PEACE together with Liquid Telecom and Africa Data Center signed a landing Party Agreement (LPA) for a landing port in Kenya, said Frederick Chui-Chief commercial officer of the PCCW Global.

CHINESE LOANS TO AFRICA

Since 2000, China has provided US$153 billion loan to African countries and most of them after 2010. According to SAIS-China-Africa Research Initiative, China's total loans to Africa from 2000 to 2018 is US$148 billion, and mostly in large scale infrastructure projects. The Chinese loan amount is gradually increasing in the past 5 years with a rate of US$2 billion per year, and 66% of the loan goes for transportation and energy. From 2016 to 2018, China's investment in Africa has doubled from US$2.4 billion to US$5.4 billion.[18] From 2012 to 2017, Chinese loans to Africa increased from less than US$1 billion per year in 2001 to more than US$10 billion in 2017. Since 2010, Chinese financial institutions have funded an average of 71 projects each year in Africa with an average value of US$180 million, and

[17] *Ibid.*
[18] *Ibid.*

among them the resource guarantee infrastructure financing is 8%. In 2019, China provided US$7 billion in loans to Africa and it was a 30% drop from 2018.

Three African countries with Chinese loans amount of above US$8 Billion

- Angola - US$42 Billion
- Ethiopia - US$13.7 Billion
- Kenya- US$9.8 Billion

African countries with Chinese loans amount between US$5-8 Billion are:

- Congo (Brazzaville) - US$7.42 Billion
- Sudan- US$ 6.4 Billion
- Zambia- US$ 6.38 Billion
- Cameroon- US$ 5.57 Billion

There are 15 African countries with US$1-5 Billion of Chinese loans, and 27 African countries with less than US$1 billion of Chinese loans, and about 20 countries with zero loans. In 2019, China's largest borrowers in Africa were Ghana, South Africa, Egypt, Cote D'Ivoire and Nigeria. Angola holds a quarter of total debt China provided to Africa countries in the period 2000-2018, which amounts to US$43 Billion.

CHINA'S INVESTMENT IN AFRICA

From 2010 to 2014, Chinese investments in Africa sector wise are as follows: Transportation (54%); Energy (36%); Industry Mining (6%); and Communication (4%).[19] At present, China' provided finance for infrastructure projects in at least 35 African

[19]*Ibid.*

countries, and these projects involve dams, power, ports, railways, highways, water conservation and sanitation. Statistics show that in the first 11 months of 2020, China's FDI in Africa's entire industry was US$2.8 billion year on year, an increase of 0.04%. Chinese companies have signed new projects in Africa and the contract value was US$55.1 billion year on year increase of 13.3 %.

Raw materials, minerals, and metals accounted for more than 99% of Africa's total export to China. Africa will also be a biggest market for China's manufactured goods. China is investing in Africa because Africa has 2/3 of the world's mineral resources including diamond, uranium, manganese chromium etc. It will open up the raw material supply channels through infrastructure. Africa is also a huge market for China's manufactured goods.[20]

DEBT TRAPS

In August 2018, a bipartisan group of 16 US Senators cited ' the dangers of China's debt trap diplomacy --it is important that the US counter China's attempt to hold other countries financially hostage and force ransom that further its geostrategic goals. China's debt-book diplomacy uses strategic debts to gain political leverage with economically vulnerable countries. Christine Lagarde, IMF's MD, warned China's policy makers to be aware of financing unneeded and unsustainable projects in countries with heavy debt burden. Ms. Lagarde told a conference in Beijing that while BRI could provide much needed infrastructure, but "venture can also lead to a problematic increase in debts, potentially limiting other spending on debt service rise, and

[20]*Ibid.*

[21]"IMF's Lagarde warns China on Belt and Road debt", *Reuter,* 26 April 2019. https://www.ft.com/content/8e6d98e2-3ded-11e8-b7e0-52972418fec4?ftcamp=crm/email/_2018___04___20180411__/emailalerts/Keyword_alert/product.

creating balance of payments challenges."[21]

Many scholars have expressed concerns about the impact of BRI projects on Africa's debt sustainability. The opacity of Chinese loans is a potential hidden debt risk that the African countries may face in the future. It is difficult to accurately measure and predict the financial situation of African countries.

China has provided Angola with a loan of US$5 billion which can be repaid in the form of oil, and through this loan, Angola can benefit from the improvement of roads, schools, hospitals and other facilities while collateralising oil production to China. Future oil production of Angola will be mortgaged to China.

African Debts to China

According to Jubilee Debt Campaign Statistics, as of 2018, Chinese debt accounted for 20% of the debt stock of African countries and 17% of the total interest paid by the African governments. According to Overseas Development Infrastructure (ODI), China accounted for 20-25% of the total debt stock of Africa. According to public information, Africa's total debt to China amounts to US$145 billion and the debts to be repaid this year is US$8 billion, and of this amount Kenya's share is 33% of debt amount, Ethiopia's share is 17% and Nigeria's share is 10%.[22]

MAJOR LOAN DEFAULTERS

As of 2020, African countries with largest Chinese debts are: Angola- US$25 Billion; Zambia- US$13.5 Billion; Republic of Congo- US$7.3 Billion, and Sudan- US$6.4 Billion. South Africa estimated to owe China an amount equivalent to 4% of it's

[22] *Ibid.*

annual GDP. Other African countries' debts to China are Nigeria (US$3.1 Billion), Zambia, Djibouti, Republic of Congo (US$2.5 Billion, and Egypt.[23]

China's foreign debts are mainly concentrated in Zambia and Republic of Congo of about US$14 billion, which is over 10% of its total loans on the African continent, and these two countries are already facing debt crisis. African countries owing debt to China are: Uganda, Djibouti, Sudan, Sierra Leone, Angola, Congo (Brazzaville) Burundi, Nigeria, Eritrea, Togo, Ethiopia, Guinea-Bissau, Mozambique, Cape Verde, Kenya, Tanzania, Cote D'Ivoire, Zambia, Comoros, Guinea, Rwanda, Madagascar, Equatorial Guinea, Cameroon, Central African Republic, Lesotho, Mali, Mauritania, Benin, Congo (Kinshasa), and Ghana.[24]

CASES OF DEBT-TRAP

As of 2020, China has funded Kenya to build a highway and railway between Mombasa-Nairobi worth US$6.5 billion. In late December 2018, Kenya came close to defaulting on a Chinese loan to develop the Port of Mombasa and a default could have forced Kenya to relinquish control of the Port to China.

Nigerian Federal lawmakers of the national assembly are demanding a probe into China's lending practice in Nigeria and to review the code of sovereign guarantee clause in loan agreement that they consider an entrapment of Chinese neo-colonial plans.

According to the agreement, Nigeria stands to cede her

[23]"Is China creating a "debt trap" in Africa? American research institutions: no evidence", *Beijing Daily*, 24 March 2021. https://www.fmprc.gov.cn/zfhzlt2018/chn/zfgx/jmhz/t1863840.htm.

[24]*Ibid.*

sovereignty to China if there is a default in the repayment amount of US$400 million for the Nigerian National Information and Communication Technology Infrastructure backbone phase 2 projects signed in 2018. Djibouti had fallen victim to China's debt trap and let China build its 1st overseas military base there.

CHINA'S MILITARY/SECURITY INTERESTS IN AFRICA

China is evolving security engagement in Sub-Saharan Africa. In the early 2000s, Chinese troops' contributions in the SSA numbered a few hundreds. As of February 2020, China has more than 2000 soldiers and staff deployed to the UN Peacekeeping mission in the Central African Republic (CAR), DRC, Mali, South Sudan, and Sudan.[25] China has become the largest troop contributor and second largest financier of the UN Peacekeeping Operation.[26] At the 2015 Forum on China-Africa Cooperation (FOCAC), China pledged US$100 million of free military assistance to establish African standby force and the African capacity for Immediate Response to Crisis (ACIRC).

In August 2017, China established its 1st overseas military base in Djibouti. China maintains its Defence Attache in nearly one-third of the total countries in Africa, and about 75% of these countries maintain their Defense Attaches in China. According to a 2014 RAND study, from 2003-2016, China conducted 13 military exercises, 22 naval port calls and 259 senior level defense meetings with the African counterparts. China has begun military exchanges with Africa such as security professionalisation training and inviting African military officers to China for

[25]Judd Devermont, "China's strategic aims in Africa", *Devermont Testimony,* May 8, 2020 https://www.uscc.gov/sites/default/files/ Devermont_Testimony.pdf.

[26]*Ibid.*

[27]*Ibid.*

workshops.[27] In 2018, China invited military representatives from 50 African countries and the African Union to discuss defense and security cooperation.[28]

CHINA'S SECURITY ARRANGEMENTS

Paul Nantulye (2019) said China's growing military engagement in Africa is aimed at advancing Beijing's economic and strategic interests, in particular its BRI.[29] Armed Conflict Location & Event Data Project (ALLED) suggests 150 violent incidents involving Chinese citizens in SSA have occured in the past decade. China needs to protect Chinese expatriate workers working for BRI projects in Africa which is about 300,000. A number of cases of Chinese being attacked were seen in Uganda, Ghana, Lesotho, Madagascar, South Africa, South Sudan, Sudan and Zambia.[30] Military deployment provided China with a security presence in a country that remains central in its ongoing effort to extend the BRI into the Sahel and the larger western African region. China-Africa Defense and Security Forum was conducted on July 10-26, 2018. Nearly 50 African countries developed new priorities for Chinese security engagement, including combating terrorism, and piracy, and protecting Chinese nationals and economic infrastructure.[31]

CHINA'S ARMS SALES TO AFRICA

The recipients of the Chinese arms in Africa are Algeria, Angola,

[28] *Ibid.*

[29] Paul Nantulya , "Chinese Hard Power Supports Its Growing Strategic Interests in Africa", *Africa Center,* 17 January 2019. https://africacenter.org/spotlight/chinese-hard-power-supports-its-growing-strategic-interests-in-africa/January 17, 2019 https://africacenter.org/spotlight/chinese-hard-power-supports-its-growing-strategic-interests-in-africa/

[30] *Ibid.*

[31] *Ibid.*

Morocco, Chad, Congo, Gabon, Cape Verde, Ghana, Kenya, Namibia, Niger, Nigeria, Rwanda, Sudan, Tanzania, Djibouti, Equatorial Guinea, Uganda, Zambia and Zimbabwe.[32] China is selling weapons to African countries to garner business from the continent rich in mineral and energy resources. Between 2001-2008, China as transferred 390 artillery pieces, 440 armoured personnel carriers and armoured cars; 20 supersonic combat aircrafts and 70 other military aircrafts. Between 2006 and 2011-15, the imports by states in Africa increased by 19% and three largest importers were Algeria (30%), Morocco (26%), and Uganda (6.2%), and Chinese arms sales was 13% of the total imports by the African countries. Between 2008-2018, Algeria, Tanzania, Morocco, Nigeria and Sudan were the major buyers of China's weapons. Chinese weapons are attractive due to its cost effectiveness and are often less advanced than the other exporters. The low cost K-8 jet trainer is estimated to make up 80% of all jet trainer aircrafts in Africa.

In July 2018, defense officials from China and the African nations wrapped up a high level security forum and both sides expected to boost a bond for surging China's arms sales to Africa. China is actively positioning itself as a major supplier of arms to the African continent and is stepping up its shipments of weapons to conflict zones through Djibouti in the Horn of Africa.

CONCLUSIONS

China's strategic interests in Africa include a set of goals primarily economic, political and security. For the economic benefits, China is securing raw materials and mineral resources as a key interest in Africa. Second, China is investing on Africa's infrastructure is an option but not an opportunity for the

[32] *Ibid.*

continent. In the process of developing Africa's infrastructure, China provides opportunities to their financial institutions, domestic investors, construction or engineering companies, Chinese workers in the continent. All these Chinese players sent to Africa for developing infrastructure makes huge profits and once the infrastructure becomes economically viable the Chinese financial institution begins to recover the loans provided with interests. So, in this way, Africa is left with an infrastructure which certainly will beneficial for them once the Chinese recovers all theirs invested money with interests and profits along with their economic as well as political presence in the continent.

China's deepening political relations with Africa is basically to ensure the PRC's stronger position at the United Nations or at any other multilateral forums with large number of African member countries. Stronger relations at the government level help China to push its economic and security agendas in the respective Africa country. China's defense & security engagements with Africa is to provide security of the Chinese citizens, investments and to achieve a sustained stable environment in the continent for the smooth and rapid expansion of the China's economic interests. Also, China looks at Africa as a major military logistics support base for expanding their security range in the Middle East, Mediterranean and Arabian Ocean.

In short, China's plan in Africa is exploitative in nature, and the African population will be converted into consumers of Chinese products; African land will be a Chinese designed economic arrangement that will sustain Chinese economic interests as well as their presence; African governments will become the caretakers of the Chinese economic and political interests if they fail to negotiate the Chinese in their favour;

African Ports and African Armies will play a supportive role in securing and sustaining the Chinese stakes and people; and the African mineral resources & oil will remain to be the engine of China's rapid economic growth.

Belt & Road Initiative (BRI) is Xi Jinping's pet project to replace the US with the People's Republic of China as the number one economy in the world, and Africa is the significant leg of the BRI for China to achieve their target of economic superpower.

(Dr. Abhishek Darbey is a Research Associate at Centre for China Analysis & Strategy (CCAS), New Delhi.)